5450IO

72

ACUPUNCTURE

An introduction to the phil
medicine, an explanation of
description of what happens
acupuncture and a review of ...e ailments that can be helped
by acupuncture.

By the same author

Allergy and Intolerance
A Complete Guide to Environmental Medicine

Modern Chinese Acupuncture
A Review of Acupuncture Techniques
as Practised in China Today

ACUPUNCTURE

Its Place in Western Medical Science

by

G. T. Lewith
M.A., M.R.C.G.P., M.R.C.P.

Green Print 1998

First published 1982 by Thorson Publishers Limited
Republished by Green Print 1998

Green Print
an imprint of The Merlin Press
2 Rendlesham Mews Rendlesham
Suffolk IP12 2SZ

© George T. Lewith 1982

All rights reserved. No part of this book may be reproduced or utilized in any form or by any means, electronic or mechanical, including photocopying, recording or by any information storage and retrieval system, without permission in writing from the Publisher.

British Library Cataloguing in Publication Data

Lewith, G. T.
  Acupuncture
  1. Acupuncture
  I. Title
  615.8′92   RM184

  ISBN 185425 091 4

Printed in Finland by WSOY

Contents

For Nicola

I should like to thank Constance Knight for her excellent work on the manuscript.

I should also like to thank Dr J. Kenyon and Dr T. Jewell for their helpful and thoughtful suggestions.

Introduction

The purpose of this book is to give an introduction to the philosophy of acupuncture and to review the current developments in this system of medicine. The initial chapters deal with acupuncture treatment generally—indicating its successes in a variety of common diseases—and there then follows an account of its evolution and history both in China and the West.

Throughout, the book is addressed to the lay reader. It neither pretends to be an acupuncture textbook nor to describe how to carry out acupuncture, but it does summarize the available information on acupuncture and what can be achieved by this form of therapy.

Within the field of acupuncture there are those who believe that their own ideas are the only correct approach to this type of treatment, so I have attempted to describe, in a balanced and systematic manner, the use and abuse of all the currently available theories concerned with the practice of acupuncture.

I do not hold to any one particular approach, but feel that all the ideas within the field should be understood, evaluated and used to benefit those who seek help. Acupuncture is growing in popularity and importance, and as it becomes more acceptable it is gradually being integrated into the fabric of Western medicine.

How to Obtain Acupuncture Treatment
Before going to an acupunturist it it wise to discuss your

problem with your own general practitioner. It may be that acupuncture is not the best treatment for your complaint and a diagnosis should be made before any treatment is given. Your general practitioner can then refer you to an acupuncturist if this type of treatment is indicated. However, the patient is the final arbiter of the type of health care he wishes to receive and ultimately the decision is his, whatever professional advice he may receive.

There are two groups of people practising acupuncture in the United Kingdom; non-medically qualified acupuncturists, and those who also have a medical degree.

There are several organizations that cater for non-medically qualified acupuncturists. Two of the main ones are the British Acupuncture Association and the Traditional Acupuncture Society. A request from any member of the general public, to these organizations, will usually secure a list of the acupuncturists affiliated to them. Most non-medically qualified acupuncturists have completed an acupuncture course; however, it is quite legal (in the United Kingdom) to practise acupuncture without any form of training, in either acupuncture or Western medicine. It is therefore wise to assure yourself that the acupuncturist you wish to visit does have some sort of formal training or qualification in acupuncture.

The British Medical Acupuncture Society is the only organization in the United Kingdom that caters for medically qualified acupuncturists. The general public is not able to obtain lists of medically qualified acupuncturists, but this list is available to doctors, via the British Medical Association, if they wish to refer a patient for acupuncture.

1. The Conceptual Basis of Traditional Chinese Medicine

One of the major assumptions inherent in traditional Chinese medicine is that disease is due to an internal imbalance of Yin and Yang; therefore disease can be treated by correcting the Yin Yang imbalance, thereby returning the body to a healthy state. Western medicine tends to approach disease by assuming that it is due to an external force, such as a virus or bacteria, or a slow degeneration of the functional ability of the body. Both Chinese and Western concepts are valid alternatives. Although this chapter is devoted to the philosophy of traditional Chinese medicine it is useful to start by examining briefly some of the assumptions and philosophies of Western medicine. This will provide a useful comparative basis which will elucidate the understanding of both systems.

Western medicine is based on the Cartesian philosophy that the body represents one functioning system and the mind another. It accepts that each system may affect the other, but essentially it sees disease as either physical or mental. The Chinese assume that the body is whole, and each part of it is intimately connected. Each organ has a mental as well as a physical function, as will be discussed later.

Until fairly recently most Western doctors and pharmaceutical companies have worked on the basis that there is 'a pill for every ill'. The philosophical approach behind this idea is that an external force, or chemical, can cure disease, but although some pills are of great value, both the general public and the medical profession have become considerably more sceptical about the widespread use of such chemicals. Traditional Chinese medicine states that the body has the potential to cure its own diseases if pushed (or needled) in the correct way.

Some authors, such as Ivan Illich, have been hypercritical of Western medicine and thus some people have looked upon acupuncture as not just an alternative but a superior system of medicine. Acupuncture is just another medical system, with ideas that may be of benefit to the individual patient and Western medicine as a whole, but it cannot be promulgated as either superior or a cure all. The major disadvantage of Western medicine is that it has the potential to cause a great deal of harm. Acupuncture, on the other hand, is most unlikely to cause any serious damage as it is a particularly safe form of therapy; this is undoubtedly one of its main advantages.

Even though the traditional Chinese explanations for acupuncture are somewhat enigmatic to the Western doctor, acupuncture does seem to have a clearly validated scientific basis. In spite of their radically different philosophical assumptions it is wiser to look at these two medical systems as mutually beneficial, rather than mutually exclusive. Each system has ideas and therapeutic methods that can be explained both scientifically and philosophically, each can benefit the individual, and together they can broaden the philosophical and ideological basis of medicine.

The Balance of Nature
The Chinese believe that health is achieved, and disease prevented, by maintaining the body in a 'balanced state'. This concept was applied to both individuals and society at large. In individual terms the ancient Chinese physicians preached moderation in all things, such as alcoholic intake and gastronomic excess. They also stated that daily activities should include mental as well as physical tasks. The wealthier Chinese visited their doctor when they were well, paying a retainer to the doctor to keep them healthy. If they became ill the doctor lost his fee.

Such a highly sophisticated and personal system of health care is impracticable within the current limitations of Western society, but the concept behind such ideas represents a radically different approach to health and disease. The Chinese culture was also one of the first to grasp the potential within the broader field of preventative medicine. Many of these ideas were effected in the public health measures, which first began to be introduced during the Warring States period.

The body is a delicate balance of Yin and Yang. Yin represents water, quiet, substance and night, whilst Yang represents fire, noise, function and day. The two are polar opposites and because of this one must be present to allow the other to exist; for instance, how can you experience joy if you do not understand misery? The state of the body is determined by the balance of Yin and Yang within it. Each of the organs of the body has an element of Yin and Yang, although one organ may be more Yang in its nature, whilst the other is more Yin. One organ may be more important in its substantive form (Yin) whilst another is more important because of its functional abilities (Yang). When the healthy body is examined as a complete functioning system the Yin and Yang properties within it are in a fluctuating balance.

The balance of Yin and Yang is not always exact. Sometimes a person's mood may be more fiery, or Yang, whilst at other times he may be quieter and therefore more Yin. Normally the balance changes from hour to hour and day to day, but if the balance is permanently disordered, for instance if Yin consistently outweighs Yang, then the body is unhealthy and disease results.

The Therapeutic Application of Yin and Yang
When there is imbalance external agents can invade the body and cause disease, these external agents being called pathogens. The essential principle of Chinese traditional medicine is to decide on the exact nature of the imbalance between Yin and Yang, and the pathogen causing the trouble, and then to correct these pathological processes. As the natural forces of the body return to a normal balance the disease is then cured.

The art of traditional Chinese medicine is to particularize the imbalance accurately so that it can be corrected quite specifically. The patient is then treated by using specific acupuncture points on the body, or the ear, in order to re-balance the body. This broad system of traditional medicine applies to all aspects

The 'T'ai Chi t'u'; the Chinese symbol representing the balance of Yin and Yang.

of therapy used by the ancient Chinese, particularly acupuncture and herbal medicine.

The diagnostic and therapeutic principles of Yin and Yang and the pathogens are based on a system of anatomy and physiology peculiar to traditional medicine. The anatomy of traditional medicine is represented by the acupuncture points and the channels that connect them. The physiology is represented by the organ functions that are outlined in the *Nei Ching Su Wen*,[1] and will be discussed later in this chapter.

The Anatomy of Traditional Chinese Medicine

The channels are a system of conduits that carry and distribute Qi, or vital energy, throughout the body. Each of the organs of the body is represented by a channel, and diseases of a particular organ can be treated by using acupuncture points on the channel representing that organ.

Disease is present when the flow of vital energy through the channels is disrupted. This may occur when the integrity of the channels themselves is damaged by a sprain or strain. The Chinese describe this as a disease of 'Bi', or pain, caused by a localized disruption to the flow of Qi. The flow of Qi through the channels may also reflect the result of internal disease; for instance, if there is a disease of the liver then the flow of Qi through the liver channel will be abnormal.

The concept of channels exists exclusively in traditional Chinese medicine. Many of the facts handed down to us by the ancient Chinese do seem to have scientifically explicable reasons, but their ideas about the channels have eluded any explanation, so far. A variety of research workers have tried to correlate the channels with nerve pathways or muscle groups in the body, but all these explanations are inadequate. In spite of their elusiveness the channels represent a practical working system for acupuncture and are therefore still useful.

Acupuncture points are quite specific areas on the channels. They represent points of maximum influence on the flow of vital energy, or Qi, through the channels. This can be demonstrated clinically by thinking about the disease process that occurs when someone tears a muscle. The traditional Chinese explanation for

---

[1] The *Nei Ching Su Wen* is the first known acupuncture text (see page 19).

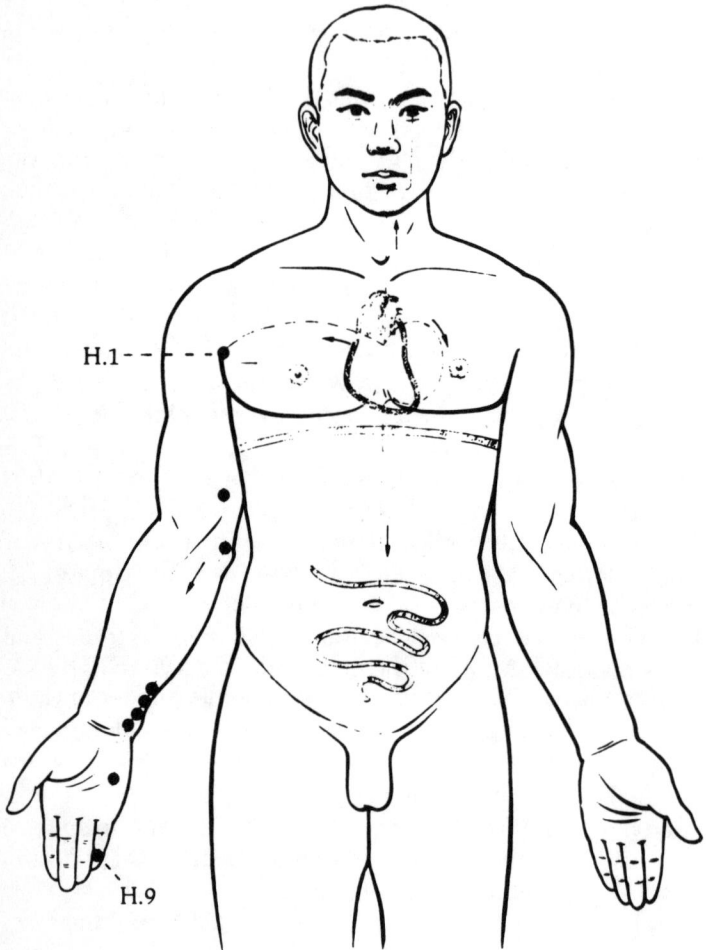

H.1

H.9

The heart channel from *An Outline of Chinese Acupuncture*.

this disorder is that the channel running through the damaged muscle has been physically disrupted, resulting in local pain, a disease of Bi. In order to treat the pain, the integrity of the channel and the flow of vital energy through the channel, must be restored. This can be achieved by the selective use of acupuncture points on the damaged channel, which restores the flow of Qi and relieves the pain.

If the internal balance of Yin and Yang is seriously disrupted (so that disease results), then there will be an abnormal flow of Qi, or vital energy, through the channel representing the diseased organ. The diseased organ must be diagnosed and then acupuncture points can be selected from the relevant channel. The use of these specific acupuncture points corrects the flow of Qi in the channel and this, in turn, has an effect on the diseased internal organ. The overall result of this therapy is to correct the imbalance within the body, and thus heal the disease; an internal disease can therefore be treated by external means.

The Chinese Biological Clock
Vital energy flows through the channels in a well defined circadian rhythm.

As the diagram overleaf shows, vital energy, or Qi, flows through the stomach channel in the early part of the day. A recent French survey showed that an accident driving to work is much more likely if breakfast has been missed. The ancient Chinese would explain this by saying that the energy required by the stomach, during the morning, has not been absorbed and therefore the body is not in a healthy state because it has 'missed breakfast'. Perhaps the idea of a large English breakfast' is more healthy than previously supposed.

The lung channel is dominant between 3.00 a.m. and 5.00 a.m. If there is a disease of the lung it should manifest itself at these times, as indeed it does; the worst time for a sufferer from bronchial asthma is usually in the early hours of the morning.

The circulation of Qi represents the traditional Chinese view of the biological clock within all of us, and, in the light of current medical knowledge, it is interesting to note how accurate are some of their observations.

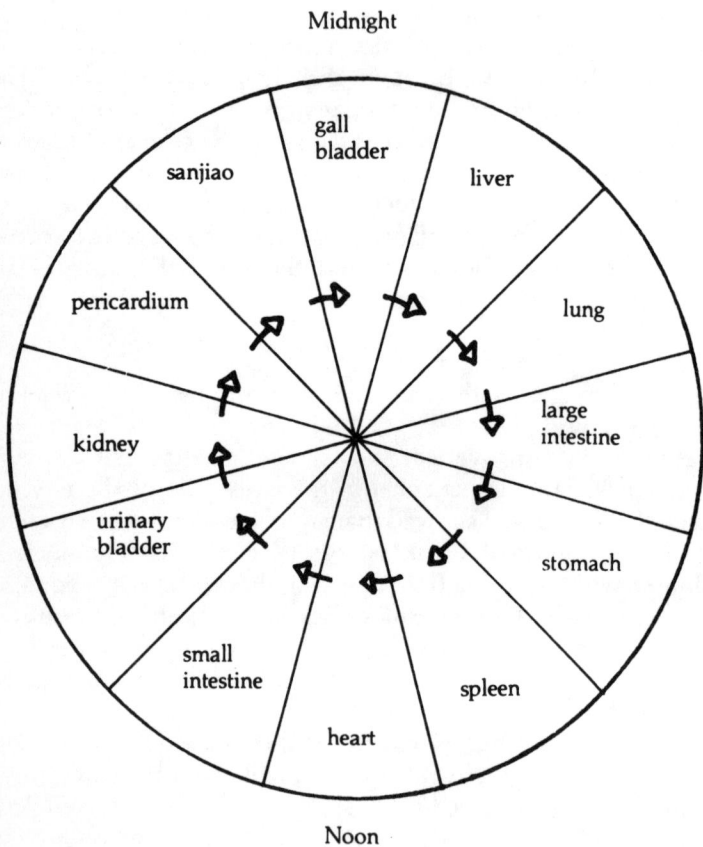

The circulation of Qi in its circadian rhythm.

The Physiology of Traditional Chinese Medicine

The physiology of traditional Chinese medicine has many similarities to that of Western medicine. Most of the specific organ functions defined in the *Nei Ching Su Wen* are astonishingly accurate in the light of modern scientific discoveries.

The heart is said to dominate the circulation of the blood. The *Nei Ching Su Wen* says, 'The heart fills the pulse with blood . . . and the force of the pulse flows into the arteries and the force of the arteries ascends into the lungs'. This seems to be a clear description of the circulation of the blood through the body, via the lungs. The idea that blood circulated in this way was peculiar to Chinese medicine until it was 'rediscovered' by William Harvey in the early seventeenth century. The publication of Harvey's work *Du Motu Cordis* has subsequently been hailed as one of the great landmarks of Western medicine, although at the time Harvey was thought to be mad, 'inflaming the medical profession by the suggestion of such a preposterous idea'.

The *Nei Ching Su Wen* also makes some surprising observations about the kidneys. It states that the kidneys dominate bone, that they play an integral part in the process of growth and reproduction (in fact the Chinese character for kidney and testicle is sometimes indistinguishable) and that the kidneys control body fluid in concert with the lungs.

During the last forty years it has become obvious that vitamin D is a very important factor in bone growth, and if it is not present then rickets results. The exact mechanism of this disease process was unclear as it was not really understood how vitamin D actually worked, but recently it has been shown that the kidney provides the missing link in the control of bone growth and development, by changing the chemistry of vitamin D. The idea that the 'kidney dominates bone' is therefore an accurate, detailed, complex and surprising observation to have been made some 2,500 years ago.

Embryology is the study of the growth and development of the foetus in the mother's womb. With the advent of good microscopic technique, in the early part of this century, embryology developed apace. It has been shown, quite conclusively, that both the ovaries and the testicles develop from the same original cells as the kidney. This process begins when the foetus is about five weeks old, (when a baby is born it is said

有竅多寡不同心導引天真之氣下無透竅七
通乎吾只有四系以通四臟頭外有赤黃裹脂
是為心包絡心
不有膈膜與脊
脅周迴相着遮
蔽濁氣使不得
上薰心肺所謂
膻中也。

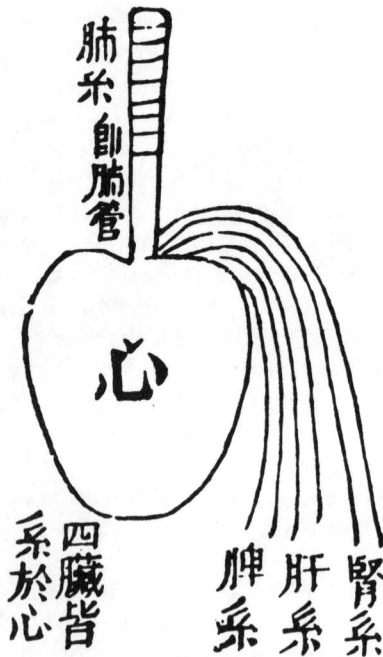

肺系即肺管

心

四臟皆系於心

腎系

肝系

脾系

The functions of the heart from *Ling Shu Su Wen Chieh Yao*.

to be in its fortieth week of development). The kidneys therefore, do seem to play an important part in the process of growth and reproduction.

The detailed and specific control of body fluid is a very complex chemical system, and one that we are only just beginning to understand properly, but it is quite obvious that the kidney and the lung do work together to control the fluid in our bodies. Most of this information has become available since the Second World War, with the development of complex and expensive machines to look at small changes in the chemicals and fluid within the body.

Communication Problems

The *Nei Ching Su Wen* contains a vast array of medical knowledge, much of which has been hidden from the West by the Chinese language, and it was not until this text was translated that the information became freely available. Many of the observations and rules within the *Nei Ching Su Wen* are based on the intricate and detailed observations made by the Chinese physicians. It does not seem to be part of the cultural make-up of Western societies to use this time-consuming method of gaining knowledge. Often we tend to be too impatient to 'waste time' observing petty detail, seeming to pursue instead the idea of scientific 'break-throughs', although, in the end, both approaches yield the same answer. One of the major precepts of Taoism is that if the individual waits and watches the 'Way' will become clear. In the West we are motivated to search actively for the answer and therefore the 'Way' sometimes takes far longer to become clear. This is well illustrated by medical concepts contained in the *Nei Ching Su Wen*, and their subsequent rediscovery.

The Five Zang Organs

Although many organs have the same functions as in Western medicine there are also radical differences between the Western and Chinese systems. In traditional Chinese medicine the major functions of the body are built around the five main organs which are the heart, the lungs, the kidneys, the liver and the spleen. In Western medicine these organs are important, but not to the same extent as in traditional Chinese medicine. The

Chinese call them the five Zang or five solid organs, and the system of the five Zang organs controls the main Yin Yang balance of the body.

Each of the Zang, or solid, organs is linked to a hollow or Fu organ. For instance, the kidney is linked both structurally and functionally to the urinary bladder. In Eastern and Western medicine both organs control the production and passage of urine. The channels representing the kidney and urinary bladder are also 'paired' as Qi is said to flow from one channel to the other. The liver and gall bladder are linked in a similar manner; they both control the formation and secretion of bile and they are also 'paired' channels.

For these specific 'paired' organs the linked functions are exactly the same as in Western medicine. The 'pairing' of the channels is particularly important when deciding on which acupuncture points should be used. Diseases of any organ can be treated by using the 'paired' channels; for example, diseases of the liver can be treated by using acupuncture points on the gall bladder channel. Traditional Chinese medicine considers migraine headaches to be a disease of the liver and they can be effectively treated (with acupuncture) by using points on the gall bladder channel.

The Emotions and Mental Disease
Traditional Chinese medicine considers that the emotions are governed by individual organs. They do not consider the brain, or subconscious, as discrete entities, therefore the body and the mind are a real part of the same functional system. Each organ is given a particular emotion; for instance, the liver is said to be the organ affected by anger. The concept that emotional functions are completely tied in with physical ones is deeply rooted in Chinese culture. In China there is less 'mental disease' as we know it in the West, because the neurotic is considered to have a disease of the liver or spleen, rather than anxiety or depression. Perhaps this explains the fallacious claim that 'no mental disease exists in China'. In my experience, having worked in a Chinese hospital, the Chinese are just as prone to neurosis as we are in the West.

There are great advantages in seeing mental functions in this way because, instead of being labelled a depressive, the patient feels that the liver is playing up and therefore perceives the disease in a different context. In the West a depressive may still be stigmatized and considered weak because he, or she, is unable to cope. In China this is not so because the cultural history and social context of mental disease is different, the depressed patient being made to feel that the disease is real and organic, rather than imagined. In spite of the constructive efforts of those who work in the field of mental health in Western nations, the body and the mind are generally still considered to be separate, and those who are unable to keep the mind under control are thought, by some, to have failed.

In acupuncture, the Chinese have a method of effectively treating a proportion of mental disease, which therefore has not been considered incurable, and there has been no necessity to shut all sufferers away in institutions. In the West most of those who are working within the area of mental disease are dealing with diseases that are poorly understood. As a general rule the level of understanding in any area of human knowledge can be judged by the number of theories that are used to explain a single phenomenon. If there is one theory that seems to explain all the facts, for a given observation, then it is probably correct. If many ideas are used to explain the same set of facts then it is likely that most of them are, at best, half truths. At present the field of mental health embraces a large number of theories which are used to give opposing explanations for the same basic facts.

Without a defined idea of the origin of disease, treatment is difficult, therefore a wide variety of poorly understood treatment methods are used in mental disease, such as electroconvulsive therapy. Perhaps the lack of social stigma attached to mental disease in China is because there has been some form of consistent explanation, and treatment, for this type of problem for the last 2,000 years. The area of mental disease is particularly interesting as I am sure that there is as much mental disease in China, if not more, than in the United Kingdom, but it would seem that the cultural and medical heritage of the Chinese people has allowed them to deal with it in a different manner from that in the West, and possibly more effectively.

Vital Energy (Qi) and Blood

The force behind the biological functions occurring in any living tissue is Qi. Qi represents the vital energy of the body but it also has a material form. It is both substance and function; the substantive or material form of Qi is oxygen (clean Qi) or food, the non-substantive form of Qi is the real but evasive concept of 'vital force'. The idea of a 'vital force' is common to many early medical systems, but it has been highly developed within the concept of traditional Chinese medicine.

If a substance has no Qi then it is dead. The Qi of the liver is the functional ability of the liver, and the Qi of the body is the total vital force of a human being. Qi is disseminated throughout the body by the channels. It is also divided into various subgroups such as original Qi, or the Qi with which you are born, and nourishing Qi, or the Qi that you gain from the food you eat. Defensive Qi is the Qi that protects the body from invasion by disease, circulating just below the skin and fending off invasion by viruses and bacteria (pathogens).

Qi is a very wide concept, difficult to understand in detail, but it is an essential part of the traditional Chinese picture of the body. Blood also exists in the system of traditional Chinese medicine, and blood production is said to be dependent on the liver, the kidney and the bone marrow. The modern medical theories on blood production also tie up these three organs as being the functional system for blood production.

Pathogens

Disease results when the Qi of the body is weakened and unable to resist the onslaught of pathogens (disease-causing factors). In Chinese medicine the agents that cause disease are given the name of meteorological conditions; an infection (often associated with a fever) is called a disease of heat, and a chronically painful joint is usually a disease of cold. These pathogens allow diseases to be grouped according to their broad symptoms. The pathogen wind is an interesting idea. Wind means a changeable symptom, so the type of muscular ache often occurring with 'flu, would be classed as invasion by wind. The idea that disease is due to physical conditions is an intuitive explanation for many common aches and pains. People often complain that 'they caught a chill when they got wet', or that their 'neck is stiff after

ORIGINAL QI
i.e. qi derived before
birth

qi of original yin
(yin of shen-kidney)

qi of original yang
(yang of shen-kidney)

NORMAL QI
i.e. qi of zang and fu
and qi of channels
and collaterals

QI DERIVED AFTER
BIRTH i.e. qi formed
from food and drink

ZHONG QI

NOURISHING QI

DEFENSIVE QI

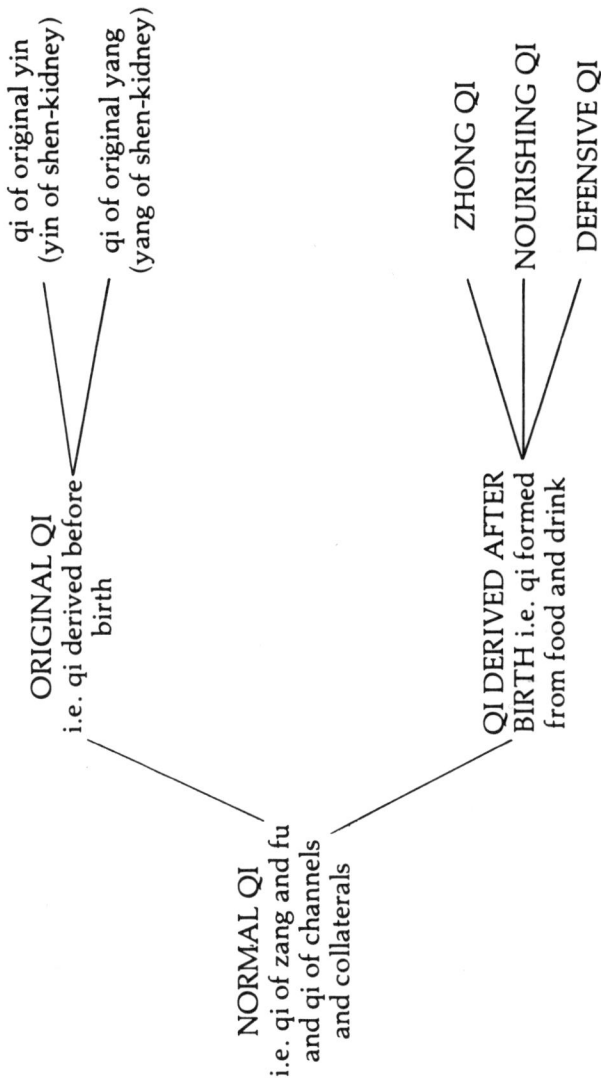

The main types of Qi that are said to be in the body.

having slept in a draught'. The Chinese pathogens represent a formalization of this approach.

A particular pathogen usually presents itself with a defined symptom complex. By using the information gained from the history of the disease, and the physical examination of the patient, it is often possible to make a clear diagnosis of the pathogen causing the disease. If the patient has a fever then heat is one of the pathogens involved in the disease process. Once the diagnosis has been made, then specific acupuncture points can be used to disperse the pathogen; when heat is the invading pathogen, then specific points are used to reduce the fever. Acupuncture points are therefore used to correct the Yin Yang balance of the body and to disperse pathogens.

If the pathogen cold is responsible for a particular disease process, then heat must be used to treat it. Moxa is the Chinese version of the heat lamp and, as shall be discussed in a later chapter, the Chinese burn the dried leaves of *Artemisia vulgaris* over the areas that require heat. Heat, or more specifically smouldering moxa, provides local heat for a variety of chronic muscular aches. It is interesting to note that the types of diseases due to cold are commonly the muscular and rheumatic aches, which are temporarily alleviated by heat lamps.

More than one pathogen can invade at the same time; if a patient is suffering from 'flu, then there will be a fever and also muscular aches that wander all over the body. This is defined as invasion by the pathogens wind and heat and, as one doctor said when I described this to him, 'the patient will be suffering from a great deal of hot air.'

Other factors may also cause disease, such as worry, or eating contaminated food. The *Nei Ching Su Wen* states that excessive grief, anxiety and overthinking will cause cancer. This idea has been supported by some recent comments in the medical press which suggest that if a woman has a breast removed for cancer she will survive longer if she is of a 'happy' disposition.

Pulse Diagnosis

For the acupuncturist, one of the most difficult aspects of traditional Chinese medicine is the diagnosis of the specific organ affected by any particular disease. In ancient China this was achieved by using a refined form of pulse diagnosis.

圖之診仰診覆

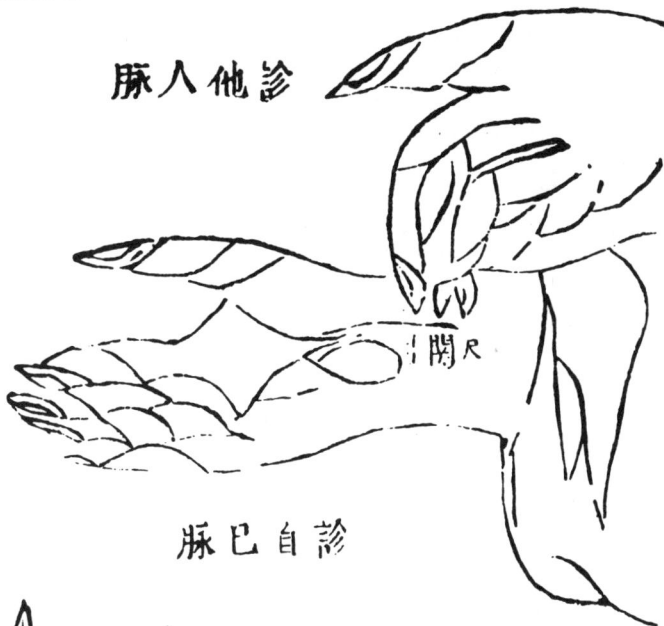

脈人他診　關R

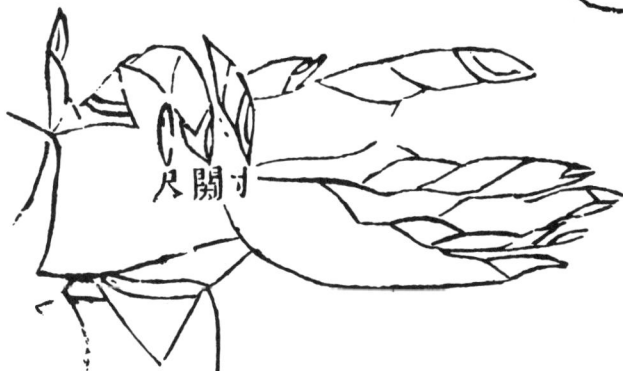

脈巳自診　尺關寸

Palpating the traditional Chinese pulses from *T'u Chu Mo Chueh*.

The palpation of the pulse enables the acupuncturist to assess which organ is diseased, whether the organ is over- or under-active, and the pathogen causing the damage. This is achieved by feeling the pulse at three positions at each wrist, and by feeling the pulse at the superficial and deep positions at each end of three positions on the wrist. There are six pulses at each wrist, three superficial and three deep. There are twelve main organs in the Chinese medical system[2] and each of these is represented by one of the pulses at one of the wrist positions. It is unclear how this system of pulse diagnosis came into existence but it was a refined and very important system by the time the *Nei Ching Su Wen* was written. This method of diagnosis allows the whole body to be assessed, and it also defines the relative balance between each of the organs. In addition, pulse diagnosis is said to give a clear idea of the type of disease process, whether it is acute or chronic, and to give a prognosis for that disease in that individual patient. This allowed the Chinese physician to give an indication of how the disease would affect the individual.

The observation that each of these pulses represents a different organ is a difficult fact to accept and understand. It is astonishing to think that different organs are represented by the pulse in the left and right hands, and that these pulses are separated only by a centimetre or so. There are also several different types of pulse that can be felt in any given position, for instance the pulse in the spleen position can be described as a 'Fu' pulse in one disease, or a 'Ch'en' pulse in another disease. These pulses were given rather poetic descriptions. A 'Fu' pulse is described as a superficial pulse, it is light and flowing like a piece of wood floating on water, whilst a 'Ch'en' pulse is a deep pulse, like a stone thrown into water.

Surprisingly enough, these pulses can be recorded accurately with the aid of modern technology. They can be printed out from a six channel oscilloscope with three pulse sensors at each wrist. In terms of modern electronics this is not a particularly complex device and allows clear graphic verification of the ideas of the ancient Chinese. The poetic description of the pulse

---

[2] The main organs are the heart, kidney, liver, spleen, lung, pericardium, triple warmer, large intestine, small intestine, stomach, gall bladder and urinary bladder.

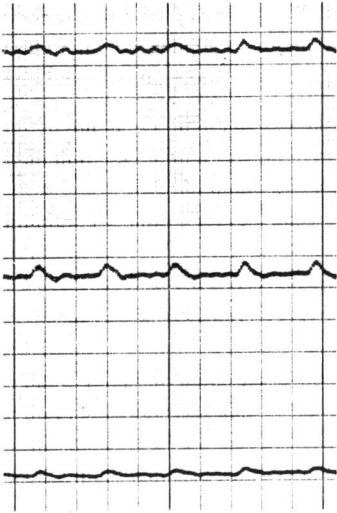

Left Superficial Pulses

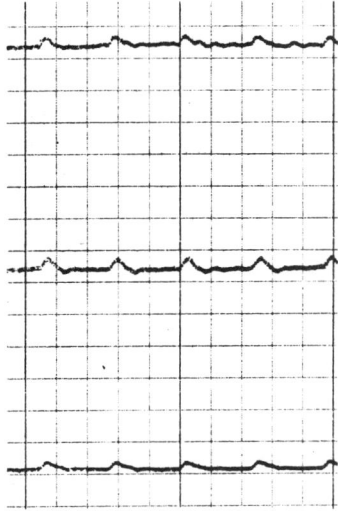

Right Superficial Pulses

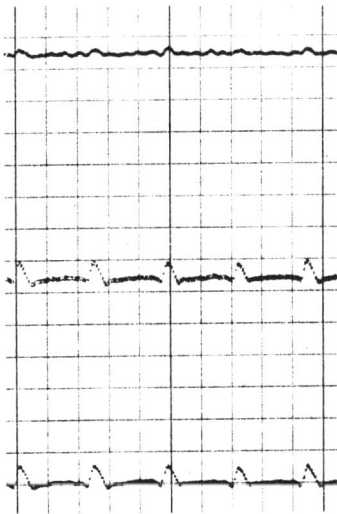

Left Deep Pulses

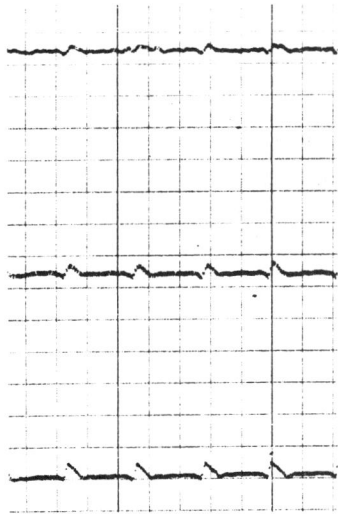

Right Deep Pulses

Pulse recordings from the pulsograph (*Courtesy of Dr J. N. Kenyon*).

characteristics also seems to be verified by the recording; a superficial pulse is indeed superficial in that there is an upward deflection of the pulse wave on the recording, and very little downward motion of the pulse in that position.

In Western medicine examination of the pulse only gives information about the rate, rhythm and volume of the pulse wave, and this information is correlated with the state of the heart and blood vessels. From the pulse recordings it is obvious that the pulse shows a great deal of variation over a small area at the wrist. It is also obvious that the shape of the pulse wave changes radically when a little pressure is placed on the artery. A superficial pulse is felt superficially and a deep pulse is felt when a little pressure is put on the artery by a finger or, in the case of the pulse-recording machine, an inflatable cuff. Although not easily explicable these facts are certainly of interest.

The Ancient Diagnostic System
Pulse diagnosis is not used in isolation, but as part of a system that involves taking the history of the disease and examining the patient. The facial complexion, smell and posture of the patient are also used diagnostically. Assessing the history of the complaint is the basis of all good medical practice, whether Western or Eastern, and can be summed up by an old Chinese quotation called the ten askings: 'One, ask chill and fever; two, perspiration; three, ask head and trunk; four, stool and urine; five, food intake and six, chest. Deafness and thirst are seven and eight; nine, past history and ten, causes. Besides this, you should ask about the drugs taken and for women you should ask the menstrual and obstetric history. Finally, for infants ask about normal childhood diseases'. This ancient Chinese system of history-taking is almost exactly the same as that employed in the West today. Pulse diagnosis was therefore included as an important part of a sophisticated system for diagnosing disease.

Modern Chinese Diagnosis
Modern Chinese acupuncture differs from the old traditional system. The old traditional system of diagnosis by the 'twelve pulses' takes many years to learn to a standard of competence which allows the acupuncturist to make a clear diagnosis. Although there are some people in both China and the West

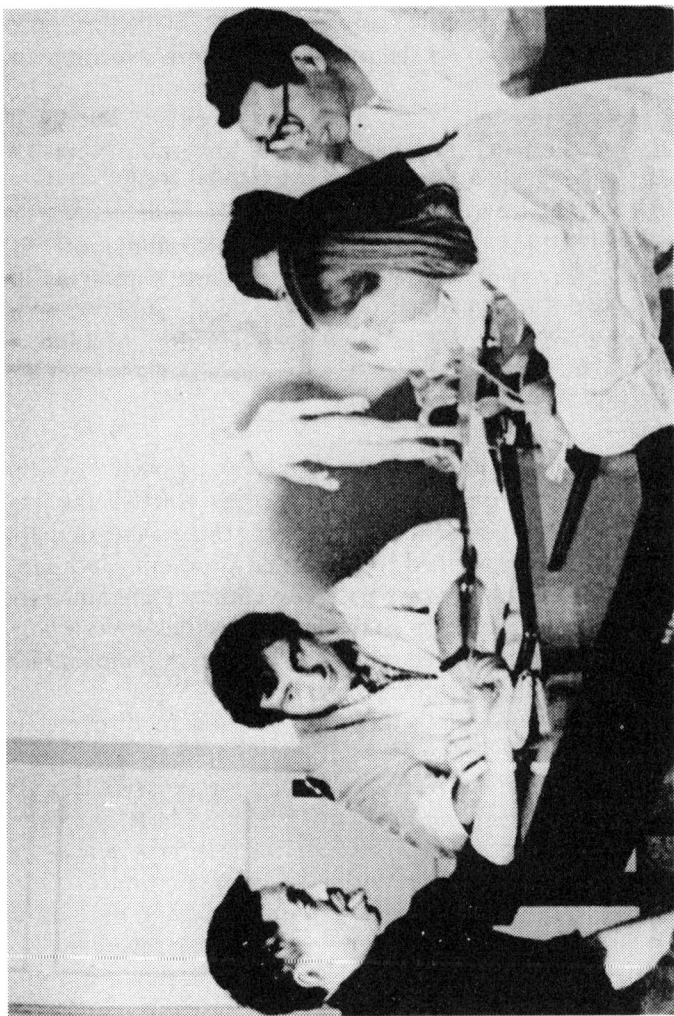

Pulse and tongue diagnosis as practised in China.

who are able to diagnose by the twelve pulses, they are few in number, and a modified system of pulse diagnosis has therefore been developed by the Chinese. This allows a simple but relatively accurate system of traditional diagnosis to be taught and practised, quite quickly and proficiently, the mainstays of this 'shorter method' being the use of a pulse generalization and the tongue.

The pulse is not felt in any particular position, but for its general character, hence the term 'pulse generalization'. The pulse can be felt at either wrist and classed as generally excessive or deficient. The tongue is also used to give quite specific information about the disease process and, in combination with the history, this system gives much the same answer as the 'twelve pulses'. Proficiency at this method will usually give the same traditional diagnosis as the pulse-recording machine, so the simplification of this system has not caused a significant loss of diagnostic accuracy.

The Selection of Acupuncture Points

The diagnosis of a particular problem does not tell the acupuncturist where to place the acupuncture needle. A set of therapeutic rules must be applied to solve that problem. To a large degree all medical systems are based on clinical experience and acupuncture is no exception to this; the rules that govern point selection are therefore based on a combination of philosophical concepts and empirical clinical experience.

There are special points that can be used to disperse the invasion of specific pathogens, such as cold or heat, and judging by some recent Chinese research work it would seem that the points used to disperse heat do lower fever. These pathogen-dispersing points are based largely on practical experience, and they form part of the basic grammar of acupuncture.

The other rules of point selection are many and varied; for example, points can be selected on the basis of the law of the five elements. This law assumes that each of the organs represents one of the five elements in traditional Chinese thought (earth, fire, water, metal and wood). They have a creating and destroying cycle.

On each of the channels there are points representing one of these elements and by applying a complex set of rules the

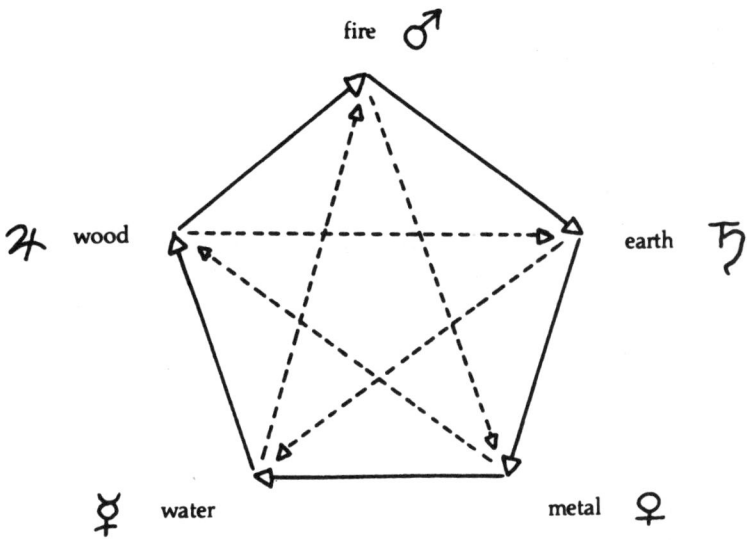

fire ♂

♃ wood

earth ♄

☿ water

metal ♀

creating

destroying

The creating and destroying cycle of the five elements.

diseased organ can be sedated, (if it is overactive) or tonified, (if it is underactive). There are also points on the back and front of the body that represent specific organs, and these too can be used to treat the represented organs when they are diseased. There is a plethora of such rules, each of which is applied in specific conditions and at specific times. The problem for the acupuncturist is to define the few points that will be best in any particular condition. The skill of point selection is based largely on clinical experience; the rules of point selection give guidelines, although they are not the complete answer.

The Use of Specific Points

Why does acupuncture need such specific diagnostic and treatment methods? Why not use all the acupuncture points at the same time? It would seem logical that if one acupuncture point helps, then two will help even more, and if all the points are used then the patient is bound to get better!

The Western doctor sometimes assumes that 'more is better'. If a drug does not give therapeutic benefit, or side effects at a given dose, then he may double the dose and the patient will probably improve. Traditional Chinese medicine implies that a small stimulus is probably more effective than a large one. Biological systems do seem to respond to small stimuli; for instance, a small change in the ecology of a 'food chain' can be amplified to cause major damage to another animal species in that environment. The emphasis in acupuncture therapy is to select a minimal number of acupuncture points in order to give the body a small but specific stimulus, as this seems to result in a better therapeutic response.

Clinical Skill

It is quite simple to practise acupuncture because it is quite simple to needle patients, but it is difficult to learn and practise the traditional Chinese acupuncture properly. It also takes some time to gain the clinical skill required to insert and manipulate the acupuncture needle. The Chinese teach that each needle inserted should be manipulated so that the patient receives a numbing or burning sensation in the acupuncture point. Many Western schools of acupuncture do not believe this and state that this sensation, which the Chinese call needling sensation, is not required. The available evidence suggests that if a needling sensation is obtained then the acupuncture is more effective, although many patients obtain adequate symptom relief without experiencing needling sensation.

Acupuncture is not a static subject. The Chinese have achieved a great deal by adapting and redefining the ideas of traditional Chinese medicine so that they are more understandable and acceptable to Western doctors. Technologically based acupuncture techniques have also been developed by Western doctors and these will be discussed in the next chapter.

2. Modern Acupuncture Techniques

If an acupuncture needle is placed in or around an area of local pain then some degree of pain relief is frequently achieved. This has led many Western doctors to use and develop this straight-forward and logical system of point selection for pain relief. Some doctors treat the painful areas alone, whilst others look at the muscle groups that run over the painful area and treat these muscles. All these methods are used by the Chinese and are described in outline in the *Nei Ching Su Wen*. These Western methods of point selection probably represent a process of rediscovery, but in spite of their simplicity they are useful and helpful to the patient. Such systems illustrate the fact that acupuncture can be effective without the use of traditional Chinese concepts, but the acupuncturist can only apply these ideas to painful conditions because there are no tender points or local painful areas in diseases such as asthma. Furthermore, it is my impression that the pain relief obtained by the patient is better, and more prolonged, if the full range of traditional Chinese concepts is used.

The great advantage of these systems is that they are easy to learn and will therefore enable simple acupuncture methods to be widely used. Many Western doctors find the philosophical concepts of traditional Chinese medicine indigestible because they do not seem to be logical, and do not fit into the context of Western medical training. It is mainly for these reasons that these adapted and simplified forms of acupuncture are an acceptable form of therapy within current medical practice.

New Methods of Stimulating Acupuncture Points
Some of the new Western ideas about acupuncture are quite radical and may represent the beginnings of a completely new approach. Acupuncture points are now being stimulated by a variety of techniques. Both Chinese and European firms have produced small electrical stimulators that allow small amplitude pulsed electrical currents to pass between sets of paired acupuncture needles. In China these electrical machines are used to replace prolonged manual stimulation of acupuncture needles in activities such as acupuncture anaesthesia. In the West, electrical stimulation is often used as part of standard acupuncture therapy. The voltage used is small and painless and is passed between acupuncture needles that have already been inserted into the skin.

As yet not enough is understood about electrical stimulation to give a clear answer as to exactly how it should be best used. There are also no clear guidelines about the frequency and intensity of electrical current that should be used on patients in any particular condition.

Biologically safe laser beams have also been used to stimulate acupuncture points and therefore to replace acupuncture needles. If used correctly these machines seem to be effective, but a great deal of further work needs to be done before they can be properly evaluated. Some researchers are also interested in the use of magnets and magnetic fields over acupuncture points, but the evaluation of these methods as a form of therapy is fraught with difficulty and is very much in its early stages.

The Pulse Reflex and Ear Acupuncture
Undoubtedly some of the most significant recent developments in acupuncture have been achieved by Dr Paul Nogier in France. The basis of many ideas that he puts forward depends on a 'pulse reflex' which he calls the Auriculo-Cardiac Reflex (ACR). This reflex is distinct from the Chinese pulse diagnosis and seems to represent a completely new finding. The ACR seems to be a method of defining the response of the body to various stimuli, but it was initially developed and used as a technique of point location for ear acupuncture.

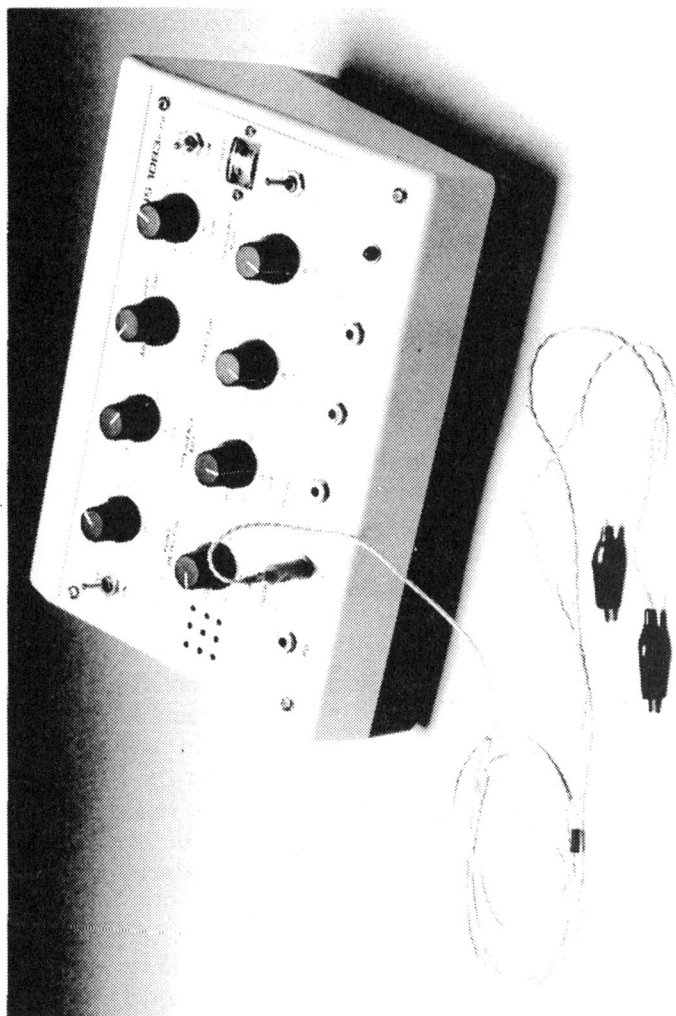

An electrical stimulator for use in acupuncture therapy and analgesia.

The human body is a sophisticated biological system, and when exposed to any stimulus it should react. It has always been difficult to prove this because it has been difficult to measure the response exactly, but ACR will probably make it possible to effect this measurement. It seems reasonable to postulate that the more advanced the biological organism then the more pressure is on that organism to respond to small environmental changes. The automatic part of the nervous system seems to be best adapted to cope with these small but significant changes in the environment. This is the part of the nervous system that allows us to digest food and breathe without thought, and is called the autonomic nervous system. If a man is being chased by a lion he becomes frightened and the autonomic system is aroused, releasing a variety of chemicals into the blood, such as adrenalin, thus giving the frightened man a surge of extra energy without extra conscious thought.

Dr Nogier has claimed that the autonomic system also changes very slightly when exposed to any small stimulus, such as light on the skin. This small change can be felt in the pulse, and this is the pulse reflex that is described as the ACR. The body is not consciously aware of all these small changes, if it was we would remain in a continual and unnecessary state of excitement; it responds and then adapts quickly and unconsciously to the stimulus.

Dr Nogier has used the ACR to develop a complete system of diagnosis and point selection for ear acupuncture. It is a system which is not based on a knowledge of traditional Chinese ideas but relies solely on the use of the pulse reflex in controlled and defined clinical situations. It is probable that the autonomic system holds many of the answers to health and disease and it is likely that Dr Nogier's work will prove to be of great significance, but at present it is not fully developed and validated.

The Electrical Properties of Acupuncture Points

A variety of electrical appliances have been used by acupuncturists to measure and quantify the skin's electrical resistance and conductance over acupuncture points, and one of the most sophisticated, and seemingly useful, is the apparatus developed by Dr Voll in West Germany. He feels that acupuncture points are rather like batteries, and the charge on the acupuncture

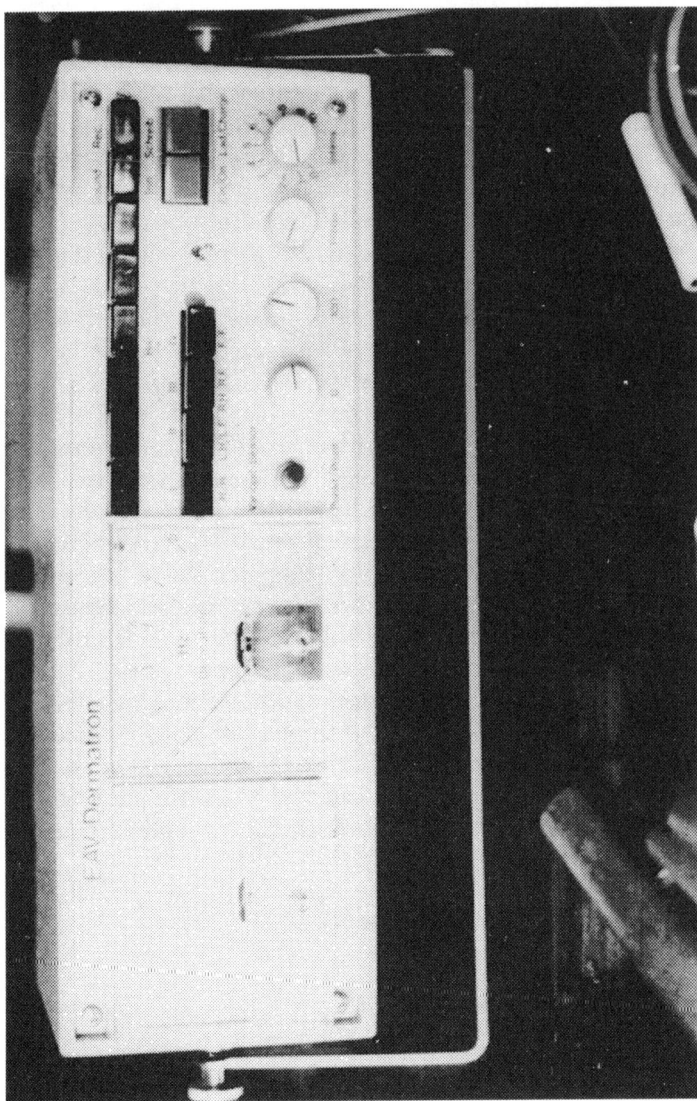

The electrical diagnosis and therapy machine developed by Dr Voll.

point represents the state of health (or disease) of the point and
the organ or tissue, deep in the body, which it represents. If the
stomach is diseased, the points on the stomach channel (these
points are on the leg), will have an altered charge or, more
exactly, an altered electro-motive force. There is a considerable
body of research work that supports these ideas and proves that
acupuncture points do have special electrical properties.

Voll's machine acts as a system of diagnosis in that it tells the
acupuncturist which points, and therefore which organs, are
diseased. It can also be used to make quite specific diagnoses as
slight differences in the charge of the point indicate different
types of disease processes; furthermore, the acupuncturist can
use Voll's machine to treat the altered (diseased) charge. Returning the point to a state of normal charge, or health, is often
enough to control and cure the internal disease process.

Dr Voll's work is firmly grounded in traditional Chinese
medicine and can be thought of as a sophisticated 'electrical
formalization' of traditional Chinese diagnosis and treatment.
There are other systems of acupuncture based on the same
principle; Roidaraku, a Japanese system of acupuncture, is
similar in idea to that of the Voll machine but is less sophisticated. The acupuncture points are measured less specifically,
but electrical measurements of the points are made and these
measurements are used as a basis for therapy.

A variety of other new acupuncture techniques are being
developed in the West, but as yet these are poorly evaluated.
China is a poor country and has little technology available, but
the West is more able to develop and evaluate these technological ideas and, at present, is far ahead of China in doing so.

3. How Does Acupuncture Work?

In spite of a great deal of excellent research designed to answer this question, as yet there are no good, clear, simple answers available. There are, however, a variety of theories that attempt to explain the mechanism of acupuncture. Pain is the area in which most research has been completed, and therefore most of the theories about the mechanism of acupuncture are related to the use of acupuncture in diseases of pain.

The Gate Theory of Pain

In 1965 a theory called the 'Gate Theory of Pain' was produced, and for this idea, and others, Drs Melzack and Wall won scientific acclaim. This theory was the first serious attempt to unify the many ideas that existed about the mechanism that perceives and transmits pain through the nervous system. The Gate Theory states that there are some specific nerve fibres that transmit pain to the spinal cord, whilst the input of other nerve fibres inhibits the transmission of pain. Both of these groups of fibres meet at a sort of 'micro-chip' in the spinal cord called the substancia gelatinosa.

The substancia gelatinosa is responsible for the integration of painful and pain inhibitory stimuli. If the pain input is excessive then pain is transmitted up the spinal cord, and the brain perceives it as pain. Pain fibres are probably the bare nerve endings found in the skin and other superficial tissues; they are easily stimulated and it would be an impossible situation if pain

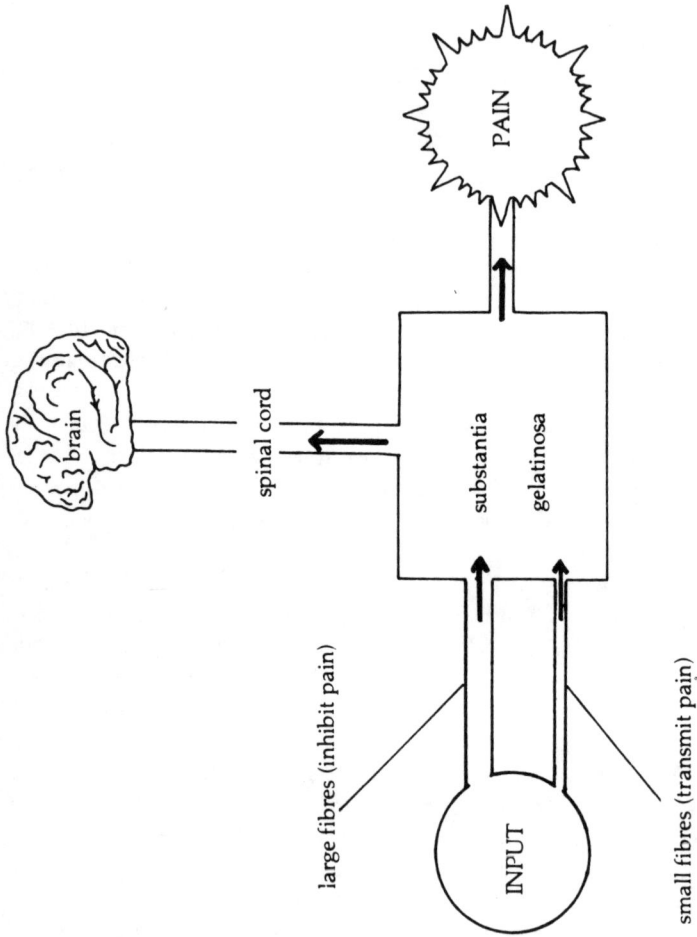

The Gate theory of pain.

brain

spinal cord

substantia gelatinosa

PAIN

INPUT

large fibres (inhibit pain)

small fibres (transmit pain)

was experienced every time we touched something. This theory proposes a balance between stimulation of the pain fibres and inhibition of that stimulus, so that pain is perceived only if the pain input overrides the inhibition of pain.

The only problem with this theory is that it does not explain fully the available facts. Acupuncture excites the pain inhibitory nerve fibres for a short period of time, thereby blocking pain, but the effects of acupuncture can last for some months after the acupuncture needle has been removed, and nothing in the Gate Theory really explains this prolonged effect. Acupuncture is a valuable treatment in a variety of non-painful diseases and the Gate Theory makes no attempt to explain the mechanism of acupuncture in the treatment of these diseases.

Another theory frequently proposed for acupuncture is that it represents a type of counter-pain. If pain is created in one part of the body then pain experienced in another part of the body is not noticed. This is a valid experimental model for short term relief of relatively mild pain, but again it does not explain the long-lasting effects of acupuncture in some types of severe pain.

Endorphins

The growing level of drug addiction in the West has provided a great stimulus for research into the mechanism of morphine action and addiction. Morphine-like substances have recently been discovered in the central nervous system. These substances are called endorphins, or naturally-occurring morphines,[1] and they have been found to be very effective in blocking pain. Endorphins are released into the nervous system by the action of acupuncture and the effects of acupuncture anaesthesia can be reversed by the use of anti-morphine drugs.

From some recent research work it would seem that not all types of acupuncture are blocked by anti-morphines. If a patient has a painful arthritic knee, and acupuncture provides relief for the knee pain, then anti-morphines do not usually block the effects of this type of acupuncture therapy. The effects of acupuncture can be very swift (in terms of seconds) and it seems that the release of chemicals might possibly be too slow a process

---

[1] Morphine, heroin and opium are all related chemicals, collectively called opiates.

to have such a swift action. The endorphin theory again only deals with pain and makes little attempt to explain the use and effects of acupuncture in non-painful diseases.

No Real Answer [2]

The fact of the matter is that acupuncture does work, and has been shown to do so, but the exact answer as to how it works is unclear. The current scientific explanations give a logical and supportable basis for stating that it does have an effect on the nervous system, but it is difficult to draw any more definite conclusions.

The mechanism of pain perception and transmission has not been clearly and completely defined, and in the light of the current state of knowledge about the basic mechanism of pain it is a little unreasonable to expect an explanation of the effects of acupuncture on pain.

The Autonomic System

It is fascinating to speculate about the mechanism of acupuncture in the non-painful diseases, such as asthma. The autonomic nervous system control's the body's breathing, heart beat and digestion. It continues to function without any conscious will, but it should not be confused with the unconscious mind, frequently alluded to in text-books on psychology. It is really better to think of the autonomic system as the automatic base or foundation on which the body is built. We understand very little about the way in which the autonomic system works, and even less about how acupuncture might affect this system.

Asthma is due to a contraction of the small breathing tubes that allow air to enter the lungs. As these tubes contract, and become gummed up, the air flow in the tubes becomes turbulent, causing the whistle or wheeze that is heard in asthma. The small breathing tubes are lined with muscle, and this muscle is largely controlled by the autonomic system. When acupuncture is used to treat this type of disease it is logical to suppose that it works through the autonomic system, and it seems possible that many of the effects of acupuncture, on diseases like indigestion and diarrhoea, work through the same system, but as yet there are no unified theories that explain either the autonomic system or the effects of acupuncture on this system.

It is quite likely that when we understand this system a little more fully we will be able to understand the mechanism of acupuncture a little better. It is also possible that the body is influenced far more by the autonomic system than we now believe. If the autonomic system is anaesthetised, then severe intractable pain can sometimes be alleviated; for instance, if severe arm pain is experienced then it may be possible to cure the arm pain by infiltrating local anaesthetic into the autonomic nerves that supply the arm. As the local anaesthetic wears off so the arm pain returns. This observation has no real explanation at the moment, because the interplay between pain and the autonomic system is unexplained.

Suggestibility
Acupuncture has been criticized for being no more than a complex form of 'hypnotic suggestion'. Available research work shows that those gaining benefit from acupuncture treatment are no more or less suggestible than those for whom acupuncture does not work. It would therefore seem that acupuncture does not depend on suggestibility. At the same time, acupuncture does have a certain amount of 'magic and mystery' surrounding it. Almost certainly this creates a small amount of benefit although it does not fully explain the dramatic and significant therapeutic effects of acupuncture.

Other Ideas
Some research workers, particularly in Russia, have suggested that fields of biological activity exist around all living objects. The concept of 'biofields' has little hard scientific evidence to support it, but there are people in both Russia and America who are suggesting that acupuncture may work through these 'fields'. Dr Nogier's pulse reflex may possibly be part of the effect of such 'biofields'. At present there are no good grounds for accepting or rejecting these theories.

The Clinical Application of These Theories
Whatever scientific theories are used to explain the mechanism of acupuncture, not one, at present, explains where to place an

acupuncture needle when the acupuncturist is confronted by a patient. The choice of which acupuncture point to use is largely based on the information obtained from traditional Chinese acupuncture, and even those acupuncturists who know no traditional theories use recipes based on them.[2] We will remain dependent on the empirical experience and philosophical theories of the ancient Chinese until a method of point selection can be deduced from an understanding of the scientific mechanism of acupuncture. Science will, and should, provide an explanation for the observations of the ancient Chinese, but in the meantime we should not reject acupuncture just because we cannot explain it completely.

---

[2] An acupuncture recipe is a selection of points used for a particular disease. No attempt is made to follow a traditional diagnosis, the points are just learnt and used automatically.

4. What Happens When You Have Acupuncture?

Some people are frightened by the thought of acupuncture and may feel that it takes a great deal of courage to inflict 'the needles' on themselves. The first, and probably the most important fact to understand about acupuncture, is that it is not a frightening experience. It does involve the insertion of fine needles through the skin, and most acupuncturists use between six and eight acupuncture needles at each treatment session. The needles used are smaller than injection needles, in fact an acupuncture needle fits into the central hole of a normal injection needle. Acupuncture needles have a dowelled end, not a cutting end like most hypodermic needles, and therefore are far less likely to cause tissue damage or bruising when inserted.

Needle Insertion
The insertion of an acupuncture needle is not a painful experience. Patients sometimes sit with eyes closed and teeth clenched asking, 'When are you going to put the needles in?', and are often surprised to learn that the needles are in place before they have finished asking the question. It would be wrong to suppose that the insertion of an acupuncture needle is devoid of any sensation, but those who experience acupuncture do not usually describe it as a painful sensation.

Needling Sensation
The Chinese state that if acupuncture is to achieve its maximum

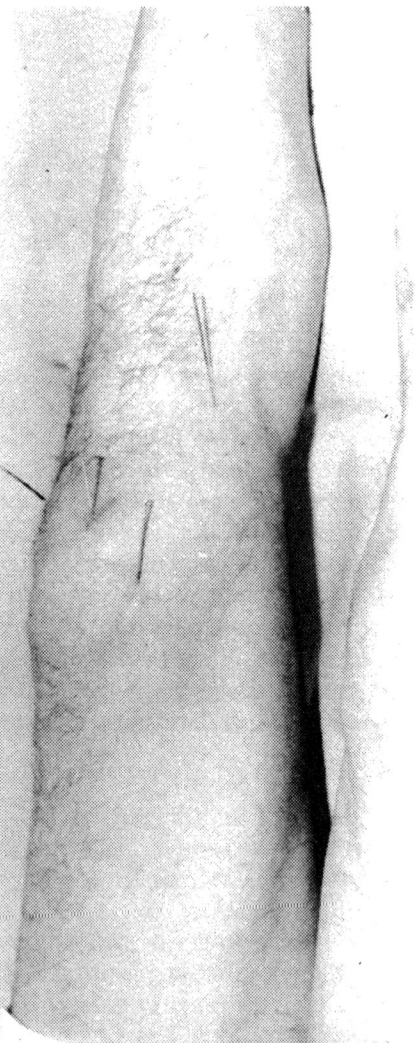

The treatment of osteoarthritis of the knee.

effect it is necessary for the acupuncturist to obtain a 'needling sensation' over each acupuncture point that is used. This involves the needle being moved slightly while it is in the skin, and the sensation experienced by the patient will vary. Needling sensation is not painful but it is a dull, bursting or numb sensation around the site of the inserted needle. The sensation may also travel up or down the channel being treated; the stimulation of an acupuncture point on the right knee may precipitate the experience of a strange burning or numb sensation in the right ankle. Needling sensation is probably best defined by the statement, 'When needling sensation is experienced the needle no longer feels like a needle!'

Some acupuncturists use an electrical stimulator to excite acupuncture points as a substitute for obtaining needling sensation. Electro-acupuncture causes a tingling sensation over the acupuncture points that are being stimulated, but the Chinese believe that this does not replace the need to obtain needling sensation. If the stimulator is mistakenly turned to a very high intensity then the patient will experience some discomfort, so it is wise to be cautious when using electrical stimulators, and to adjust the intensity slowly and carefully.

Belief

Another common misconception is that patients must 'believe' in acupuncture to enable it to work. This is similar to the idea that acupuncture is a complex form of suggestibility, but this is quite wrong. Like any other type of medicine acupuncture works on those who believe in it and those who do not. The mechanism of acupuncture is not clearly understood but, as has already been mentioned, it is quite clear that reproducable biological changes occur when an acupuncture needle penetrates the skin. Whilst accepting that all medical treatment is more effective if the doctor is trusted by the patient, this trust is not a prerequisite for the physiological changes that occur during and after acupuncture.

Will I Get Better?

No medical treatment works all the time, and acupuncture is no exception to this rule. There are many problems in assessing acupuncture as a form of treatment for any disease. First of all the doctor must have a clear idea of the natural history of the disease; if the disease is going to get better anyway, it is a little presumptuous to claim that the cure is due to acupuncture, just because the patient has received acupuncture. Furthermore a vast number of statistics must be collected and analyzed before any treatment can be adequately assessed, and in the field of acupuncture the research has not yet been satisfactorily completed. This makes the question 'What chance of improvement do I have?' a very difficult one to answer exactly for a specific condition.

In the West, the condition that is most commonly treated by acupuncture is pain and, in general, acupuncture has a significant effect in about seventy per cent of painful diseases. The results and data available about 'success rates' will be discussed in detail in later sections.

Response to Treatment

It is very difficult to be dogmatic about how a patient will respond to acupuncture. Occasionally, one treatment is all that is required, whilst other people may need a number of treatments to gain the same result for the same disease. In general most people, and their problems, do not respond magically to one treatment, and between four and eight treatment sessions may be required in order to obtain the best results from acupuncture.

Acupuncture usually works in stages. The first two or three treatments represent a process of 'understanding the needs of the patient', and are therefore a sort of experiment designed to assess the specific requirements for that person in that particular condition. Some people respond to classical Chinese body acupuncture, whilst others respond better to ear acupuncture. This partially reflects the skill of the acupuncturist in the use of specific techniques, but it also represents the fact that the body responds in a slightly different way to slightly different stimuli. Some people seem to respond to a particular acupuncture technique for one condition, whilst requiring a completely different technique for another complaint. A patient may even respond to a particular approach for a specific condition and then stop improving half way through treatment, thus necessitating an alternative approach to that condition. If a patient experiences

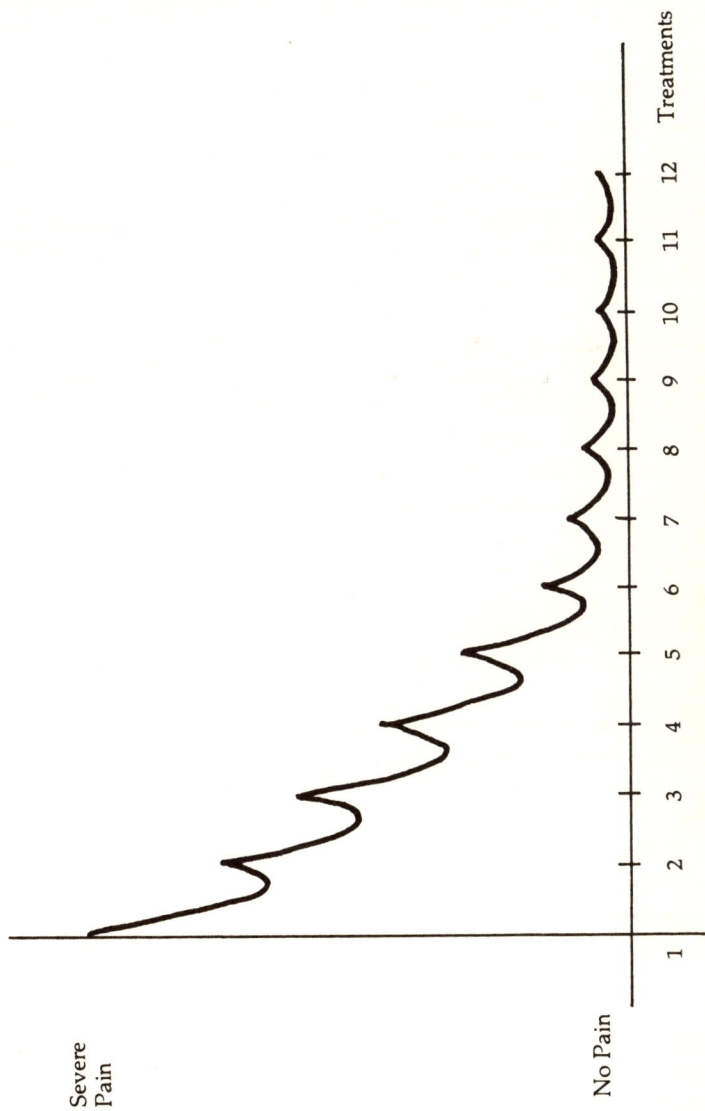

Severe Pain

No Pain

1   2   3   4   5   6   7   8   9   10   11   12   Treatments

An effective response to acupuncture treatment.

some symptomatic improvement at the first consultation, then they often gain considerable relief from a course of acupuncture; equally, many people who do not obtain symptomatic improvement at the first consultation may also gain a great deal from acupuncture. It is a good prognostic sign if there is some instant improvement, although the improvement gained at the first consultation rarely lasts longer than a few hours, and may last only a few minutes. Each subsequent treatment should then give a better and more prolonged result and, as shown on the graph, the symptoms should gradually disappear as the treatment becomes effective.

Three treatments should be adequate to assess whether a patient will respond to acupuncture. If there has been no response to treatment after the first three sessions then it is doubtful whether any response will occur. This should be taken as a general guideline and not as an unbreakable rule as sometimes the symptoms of a particular condition may be very fluctuant, and it may be difficult to obtain a clear assessment of the results of treatment. Occasionally the patient may not find it easy to remember exactly what the condition was like three weeks before and this too can create difficulties, so it is wise to keep a diary and assess day by day the changes that are arising in the problem being treated. This will allow the patient and the acupuncturist to develop a clear idea of the response to treatment, and to assess whether the treatment is worthwhile.

Most acupuncturists continue to treat a patient until there is no further improvement in their condition. The response, as shown by the graph, tends to 'level off' towards the end of treatment (usually after five or six treatments) and this 'levelling off' signifies that further treatment will probably not give further benefit. Acupuncturists in the West tend to treat people on a weekly basis; in China treatment is given daily, but this seems to be more from habit rather than for any good medical reason. Weekly treatments allow both patient and acupuncturist to gain a clear assessment of the progress and response to treatment.

Reactions
Sometimes a patient may experience a temporary worsening of symptoms due to acupuncture; this is a response to treatment and is a good sign. Such 'reactions' to treatment only last for a

short time, perhaps a day or two, and are usually followed by improvement. A 'reaction' usually means that the acupuncture needles have been overstimulated as some patients are very sensitive to acupuncture and may respond to normal stimulation by overreacting. If a 'reaction' occurs, the patient should be stimulated less at the next treatment session; this means giving a shorter and less aggressive treatment. Sometimes the improvement may be very delayed and the condition may not improve until the treatment has ceased. Occasionally patients who have been abandoned, with no improvement after three weeks, will suddenly find improvement some weeks after the acupuncture has ceased.

Although I have outlined general guidelines about the response to treatment it is important to take each problem as it arises. The general rules are not always obeyed, and if they are followed too dogmatically then the versatility of acupuncture may be lost.

Cure or Symptom Relief?
Acupuncture can be a cure, or it can act as a palliative treatment; this depends on the condition that is being treated. If a chronically painful arthritic knee is treated with acupuncture then, on average, the improvement will last about six months and the knee will then require re-treatment. Some acupuncturists treat their patients every three months or so to avoid any deterioration in their condition. The traditional Chinese approach is to attempt to maintain the patient in a state of health and a regular three-monthly treatment pattern is therefore justified; however, many acupuncturists just treat patients when the symptoms recur. If the condition is self-limiting, such as the pain from an attack of shingles, then no further treatment is required after the pain is relieved.

Whole Body Therapy
In the West the vast majority of people look upon acupuncture as an alternative treatment for pain; therefore pain is the most frequently presented complaint at an acupuncture clinic. If the patient is approached from the traditional Chinese viewpoint then the body is treated as an integrated system. People in pain frequently have other complaints, such as heartburn or

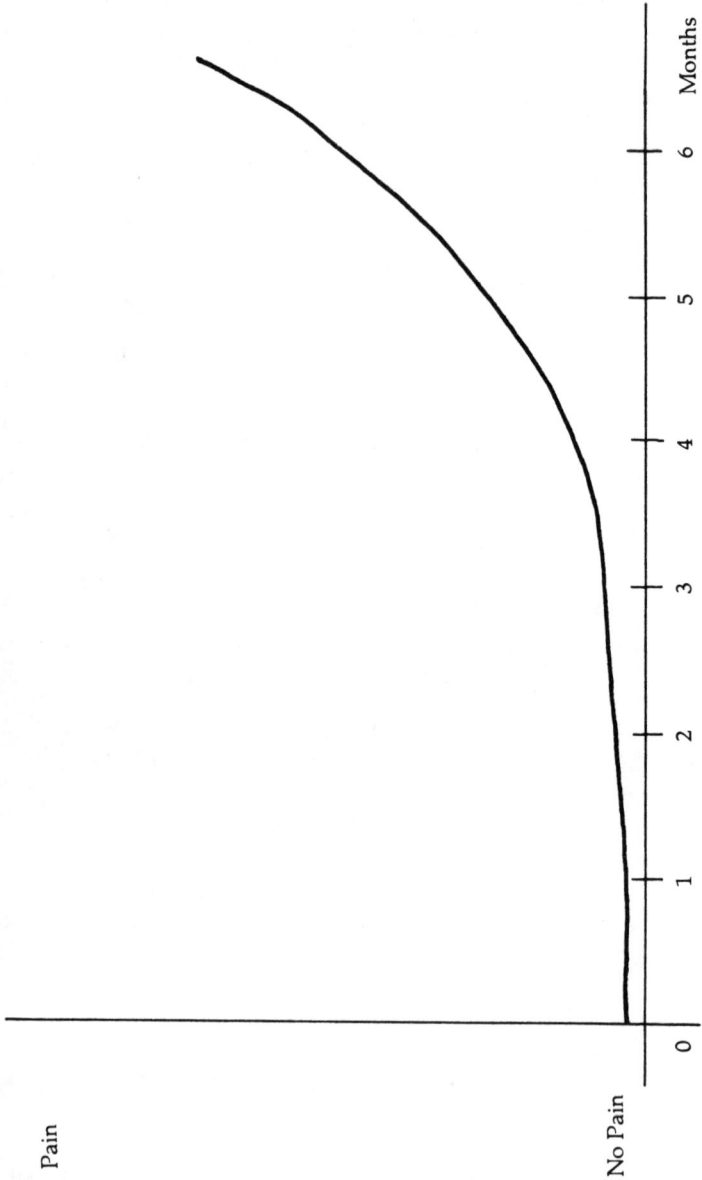

Pain

No Pain

0   1   2   3   4   5   6   Months

The long term effects of acupuncture treatment.

depression, and if the body is treated as a complete system then these complaints will also be treated, and often resolve during the course of acupuncture. The patient may be quite surprised to find that some other problem has suddenly improved, as it was not realized it was amenable to acupuncture treatment and therefore not mentioned to their acupuncturist.

5. Which Diseases Can be Helped by Acupuncture?

In the field of acupuncture few good clinical research trials have been completed, and there has also been very poor follow-up assessment of many of the conditions that have been treated by acupuncturists. It is therefore impossible to give a clear idea of the success of acupuncture in some of the conditions which will be mentioned in the following sections.

It is also essential for the reader to recognize two important facts — firstly that acupuncture, like any treatment, is not a guaranteed cure for disease. Some diseases are more successfully treated (by acupuncture), whilst others are less successful, but no disease responds 100 per cent of the time to any form of treatment. Secondly, some of the suggestions that will be made to illustrate the effectiveness of acupuncture, in particular conditions, are no more than educated guesses. Information about the success rate of acupuncture is not available in some areas, and there the only advice that can be given is based on the clinical experience of individual practitioners.

Before embarking on a course of acupuncture, whatever the condition being treated, it is wise to allow a clear diagnosis to be made. This puts both the patient and the acupuncturist in the position where the complaint can be treated properly, and the results of treatment can be assessed objectively. It may be that Western medicine offers an excellent form of therapy for a particular condition, and in that instance it would be wrong to advise the patient to have acupuncture.

Many of the facts and figures quoted in the following sections are the results of clinical trials carried out in China, so it is worth while mentioning several facts about these 'Chinese trials'. They involve the assessment of a huge number of patients, sometimes up to 10,000, but the published assessments of success and failure are often unclear, and the research is poorly designed. The Chinese also treat their patients for long periods and a stroke patient may receive one hundred or two hundred acupuncture treatments before being declared a success or a failure.

All these factors create difficulties when discussing specific diseases but, in spite of this, I have made an attempt to provide an objective assessment of the effects of acupuncture in some common diseases. It is impossible to cover the whole range of medicine in so short a chapter, so some complaints have been excluded.

It is my hope that future research work will provide information about the effects of acupuncture in a wide variety of diseases, as only with this information will acupuncture make any progress as a recognized form of therapy.

DISEASES OF THE MUSCLES, BONES AND JOINTS

The muscles, bones and joints are usually called collectively the musculo-skeletal system. When disease or damage occurs to this system it nearly always results in pain, and most people use words such as rheumatism or arthritis to describe this type of pain. Before discussing the effects of acupuncture on such pain, it is important to clarify the conditions that are collectively called 'rheumatic' as some rheumatic diseases respond well to acupuncture whilst others seem to respond less well.

There are three main types of damage that occur to the musculo-skeletal system; the first is a sudden injury or sprain which might be a domestic injury, or might be incurred during a sporting activity or in a car accident. This usually causes local pain and bruising lasting for a few days, or even a few weeks. The other main group is arthritis and this can be divided into two important types, osteoarthritis and rheumatoid arthritis.

Osteoarthritis is by far the commoner type of arthritis and can be thought of as 'wear and tear' damage to a joint. It usually occurs in older people and tends to affect the spine (both neck and lower-back), the hips, knees, elbows and shoulders. Nobody is clear about the exact cause of osteoarthritis; it can sometimes run in families or it may result from severe localized damage in earlier life, such as a broken bone. Osteoarthritis tends to develop in one or two of the main weight-bearing joints of the body, but it does not usually affect all the joints of the body. The pain caused by osteoarthritis fluctuates; if a person suffers from osteoarthritis of the knee there will be periods when the knee is painful, and other times when the pain is less severe.

The X-ray of an osteoarthritic joint looks ragged and shows some joint destruction, but such X-ray findings do not correlate with the pain suffered. If joint destruction is demonstrable on the X-ray the patient may not have severe pain, and conversely the patient may have severe pain with few X-ray findings. The main problem with osteoarthritis is pain, which in turn causes a general lack of mobility and limited joint movement.

Rheumatoid arthritis is far less common than osteoarthritis and represents a completely different disease process. The small, non-weight-bearing joints in the hands and feet are affected by an active destructive process. This process is poorly understood and can occasionally result in joint deformity.

Sprains
Sudden injury or sprains usually respond well to acupuncture. The pain resulting from a sprained shoulder will often continue for some days or weeks after the initial injury. Once a clear diagnosis has been made acupuncture can usually be used to relieve this type of pain. Many of these 'acute pains' represent a self-limiting disease process; for instance a small burn is usually excruciatingly painful for a few days and then settles. If acupuncture is used as a form of pain relief for burns then its 'pain relieving' effect is only required for a few days. Because of the natural history of the pain it is therefore difficult to produce a clear picture of the effect of acupuncture on this type of 'short-lived pain'. In China, acupuncture is usually given for acute pain, but in the West acupuncture is not generally available for 'short-lived pain' as there are not enough acupuncturists to provide this service.

The experience of a variety of acupuncturists, myself

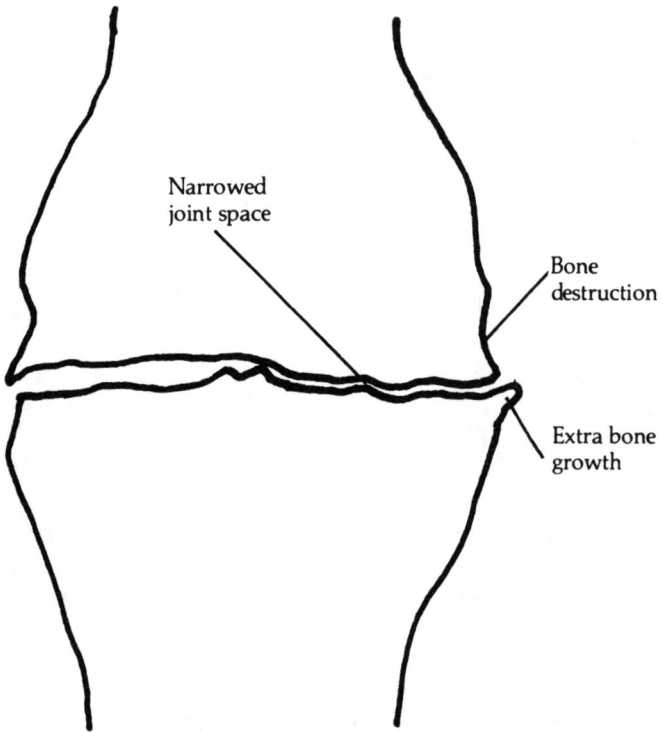

Narrowed
joint space

Bone
destruction

Extra bone
growth

An osteoarthritic joint.

included, shows that, of the people treated for differing acutely painful conditions, about 70 per cent obtain swift and significant pain relief. If a fracture of the bone is present then the pain relief gained from acupuncture is less effective than if the injury is due to a strain or tear of the muscles, tendons or ligaments. The main advantage of treating these acute pains with acupuncture is that chronic pain can be avoided. A sudden shoulder injury may produce pain and immobility for many months, sometimes years, but if acupuncture is used when the pain occurs then it seems that chronic pain may be avoided. These 'impressions' about the use of acupuncture in acute pain are consistently quoted, both in the West and China, but until adequate statistical research is completed the effectiveness of acupuncture in 'acute pain' will remain no more than a clinical impression.

Osteoarthritis

Osteoarthritis and the rheumatic pains that result from this type of joint damage, are quite a common problem. People frequently complain that their arthritic knee pain is worse in cold or damp weather and this demonstrates quite clearly the origin of the concept of pathogens in traditional Chinese medicine. The pathogen in osteoarthritis is almost always cold or damp and therefore these pains should be treated by the use of localized heat.

A great deal of research work has been done to investigate the effects of acupuncture on the pain caused by osteoarthritis. Some of this work is excellent but, for a variety of technical reasons, some is poor. Clinical trials have been completed on knee, hip, elbow, neck and lower back pain, and the information from these trials shows that significant pain relief can be achieved in about 70 per cent of those who receive acupuncture. Some work suggests that only 50 per cent of people benefit from acupuncture while other trials show 95 per cent of the patients benefiting.

The effect of acupuncture in osteoarthritic pain does not last for ever, the available research showing that its effects gradually diminish after about six to nine months. Some people may have significant pain relief for up to two years, but the majority of people who gain relief from acupuncture will require further treatment after about six months. Treatment is usually

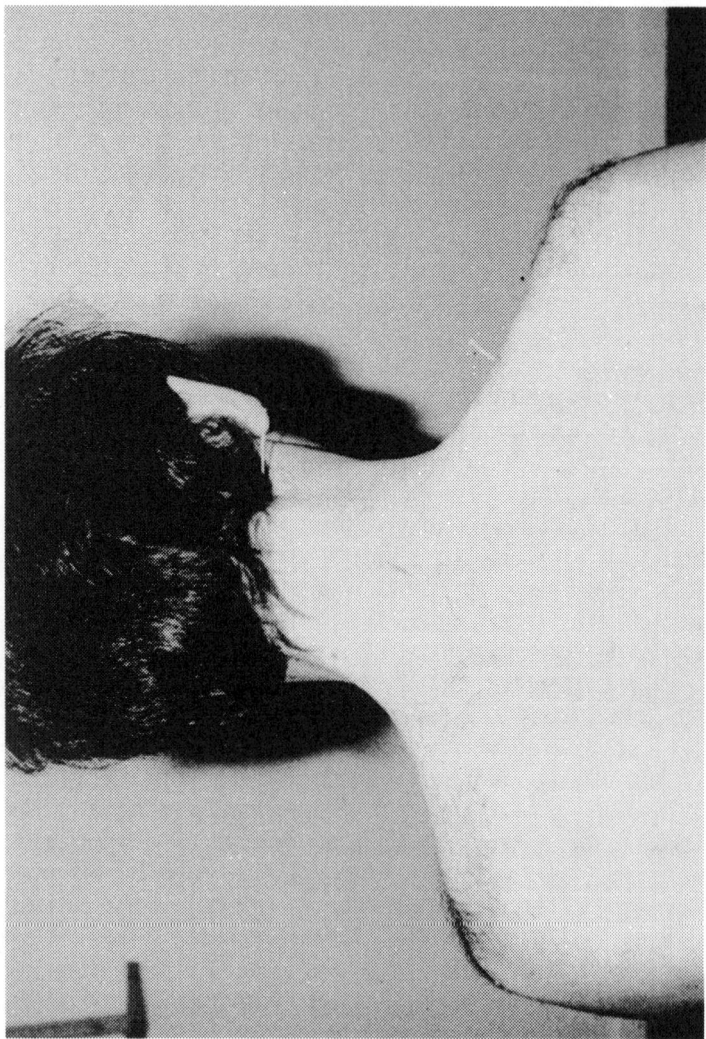

The treatment of neck pain using body acupuncture.

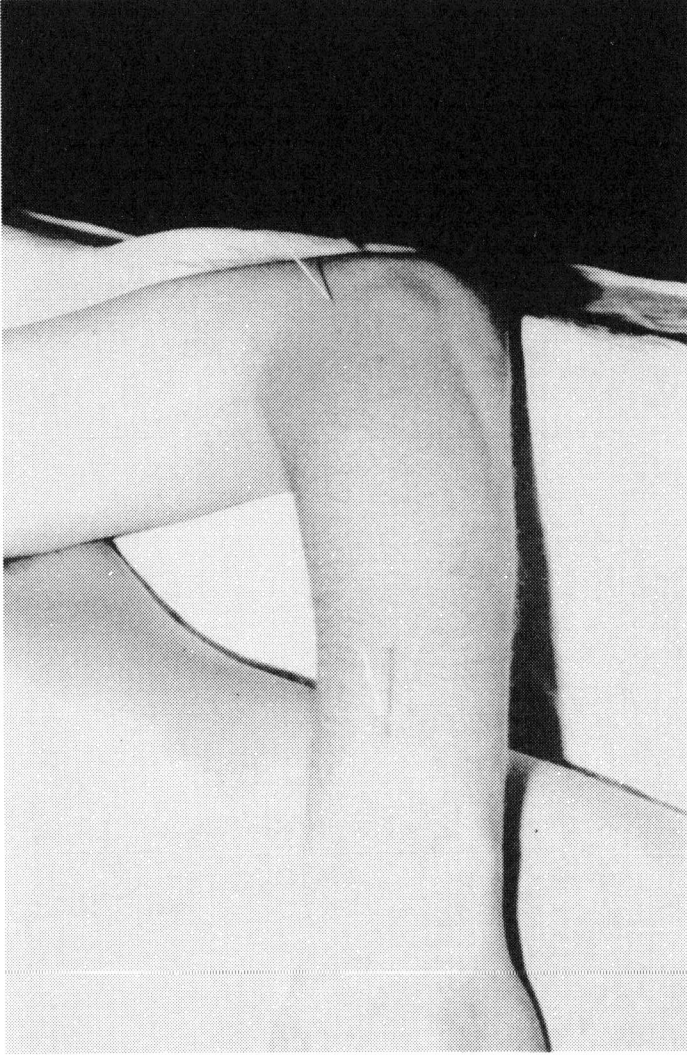

The treatment of a painful elbow using body acupuncture.

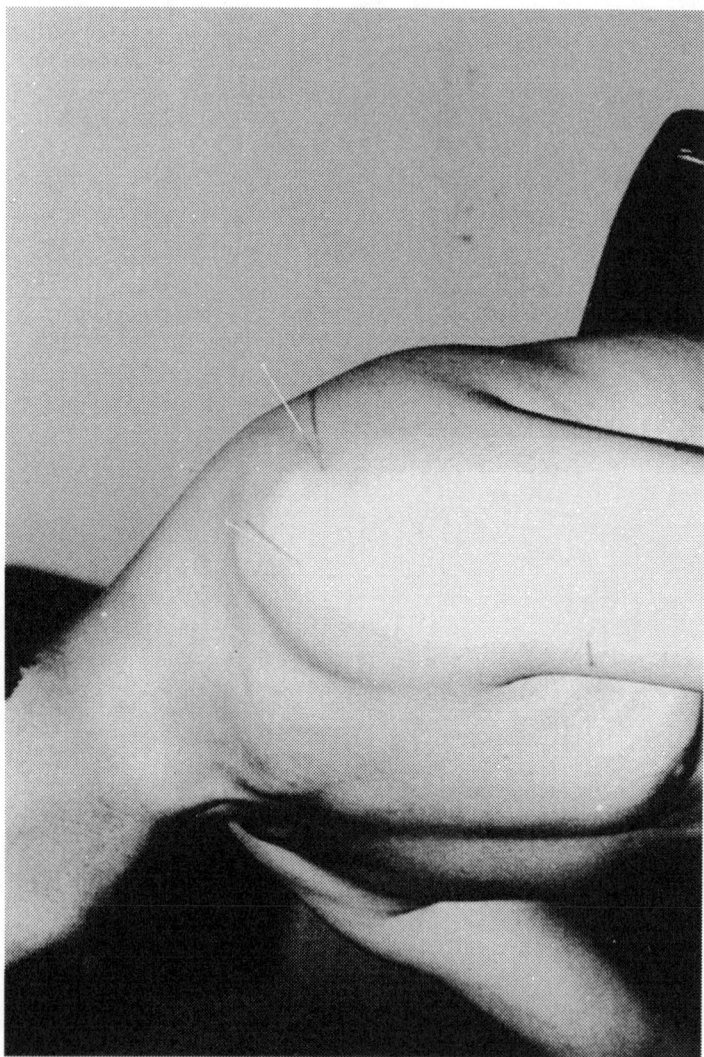

The treatment of shoulder pain using body acupuncture.

just as effective on the second or third occasion as it was initially.

Osteoarthritis is a condition that naturally causes intermittent pain and discomfort. Patients may find that their osteoarthritic knee is relatively painless for nine months and then goes through a painful period for a further six months. For this reason the effects of any treatment must be compared to the natural history of the disease process and this can cause difficulty in interpreting the results of individual treatments. Acupuncture also has a 'magical quality' that pills do not have, so it is difficult to sort out the effects of the 'magic' as compared to the real effects of acupuncture. In spite of these problems, acupuncture is a safe and effective form of treatment for osteoarthritis.

Rheumatoid Arthritis
The effects of acupuncture on rheumatoid arthritis are not so clear cut. During the early, acute, inflammatory stage of rheumatoid arthritis there is some evidence to suggest that acupuncture might worsen the pain and therefore many acupuncturists do not treat acute rheumatoid arthritis. After some months the acute inflammatory stage subsides and the residual joint destruction may then lead to the development of a secondary osteoarthritis. This type of pain is amenable to acupuncture and responds in the same way as other osteoarthritic aches and pains.

Chronic pain, due to disease of the musculo-skeletal system, is frequently amenable to acupuncture treatment. The published research shows that pain which has been present for many years can respond as well as pain that has been present for only a few months; therefore, from the available information, it is fair to say that acupuncture is 'always worth a try' in this type of condition.

HEADACHES

Headaches can be due to a multitude of factors; arthritis of the neck, dental problems, sinusitis, stress and tension, and head injury are a few of the many causes. Headaches have been dealt with as a separate section because they are so common and they span many of the 'body systems'.

Migraine is a particular type of headache and worthy of special mention. Migraine can be induced by a variety of stimuli such as foods, noise and stress, and such headaches are usually accompanied by severe incapacitating pain, nausea, vomiting, and visual patterns or flashes in front of the eyes. Many people describe severe 'tension headaches' as migraines and although these headaches are not strictly migraines, the dividing line between other headaches and migraine is frequently rather woolly. Migraine is probably best thought of as a severe headache associated with nausea.

Headaches are a common complaint and a notoriously difficult one to treat effectively, and they can be the cause of a considerable amount of distress and marital disharmony. Acupuncture has been used to treat a wide variety of headaches, particularly migrainous headaches, and the results obtained have been very encouraging. The published work suggests that between 65-95 per cent of all headache sufferers obtain significant and long lasting pain relief from acupuncture treatment. Migraines seem to respond as well as, if not better than, other types of headache.

Acupuncture therapy for headaches may cause the headaches to vanish completely, or occur with a markedly decreased intensity and/or frequency. The pain relief resulting from acupuncture can sometimes be maintained for some years and re-treatment is usually required less frequently for headaches than for other conditions such as osteoarthritis.

DISEASES OF THE NERVOUS SYSTEM

Strokes
A stroke is caused by a disturbance of the blood supply to the brain. The blood vessels that normally supply blood to the brain can be compromised by becoming blocked or bleeding. This results in a deficient blood supply to the brain tissue and these events can be precipitated by a variety of factors such as raised blood pressure, hardening of the arteries and severe head injury. The brain is divided into many different functional areas, one area controlling speech, while another dominates the sensations

of touch and pain. The functional impairment that occurs with a stroke depends on the area of the brain that is damaged; if the speech area is damaged by a lack of blood supply then the patient may be unable to speak properly.

In China, acupuncture is the standard treatment for strokes. In the West, the mainstays of stroke treatment are speech therapy, physiotherapy and occupational therapy, but the Chinese feel that these methods have less to offer than acupuncture. Both scalp and body acupuncture are techniques that can be used to aid recovery from a stroke. The research work so far completed suggests that acupuncture increases the blood supply to the brain, and for some unexplained reason this seems to improve functional ability and acts as a stimulus to recovery after a stroke.

Clinical trials completed by the Chinese state that some effect can be gained from acupuncture in about 80 per cent of strokes. These trials are difficult to interpret clearly as a significant number of stroke patients recover spontaneously; furthermore, the Chinese trials are poorly designed and the exact definition of the success and failure of treatment is unclear. The success rate claimed is very high but to some extent this success rate is mirrored by the experience of a variety of doctors in the West. Whatever criticism one has about Chinese research methods, Western medicine often has little to offer the stroke patient and therefore acupuncture is always worth considering. Ideally strokes should be treated within six months of the damage occurring. The patient may continue to benefit for up to two years after the stroke but, as a rule, acupuncture can effect little improvement if the damage has been present for more than two years.

The Neuralgias

The neuralgias are a collection of poorly understood and frequently painful conditions. The more common and clearly defined types of neuralgia will be discussed in the following section.

Trigeminal neuralgia usually presents with severe unilateral facial pain. Its cause is unclear but the painful facial spasms are often precipitated by cold or wind. The Chinese claim to be able to gain some improvement, with acupuncture, in about 70 per

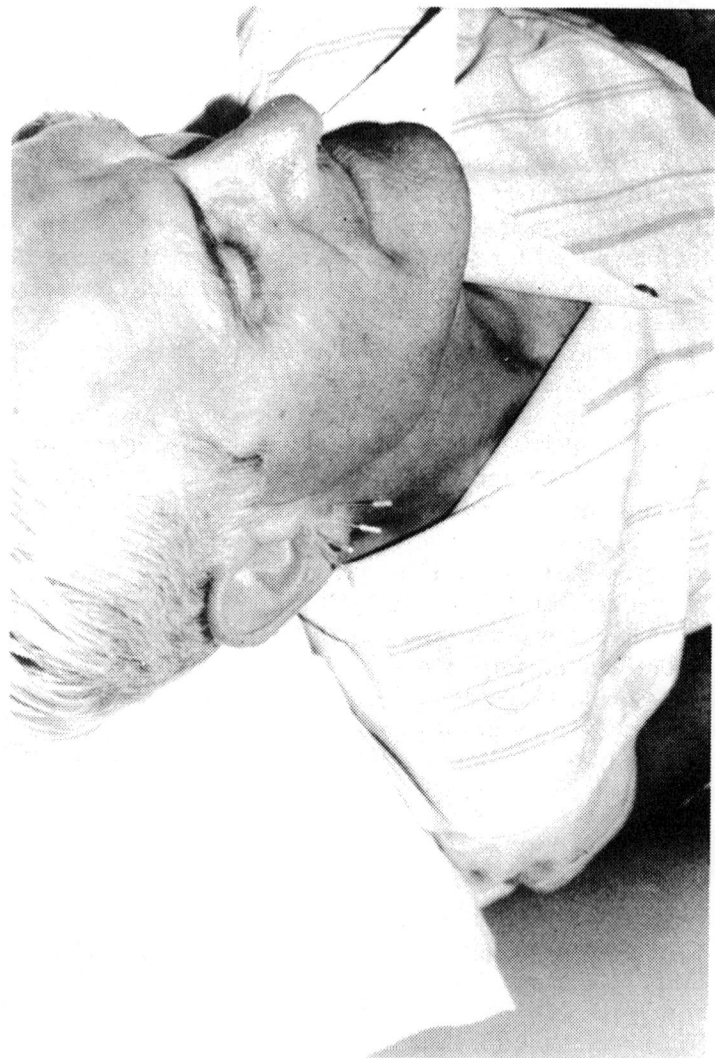

The treatment of trigeminal neuralgia using ear acupuncture.

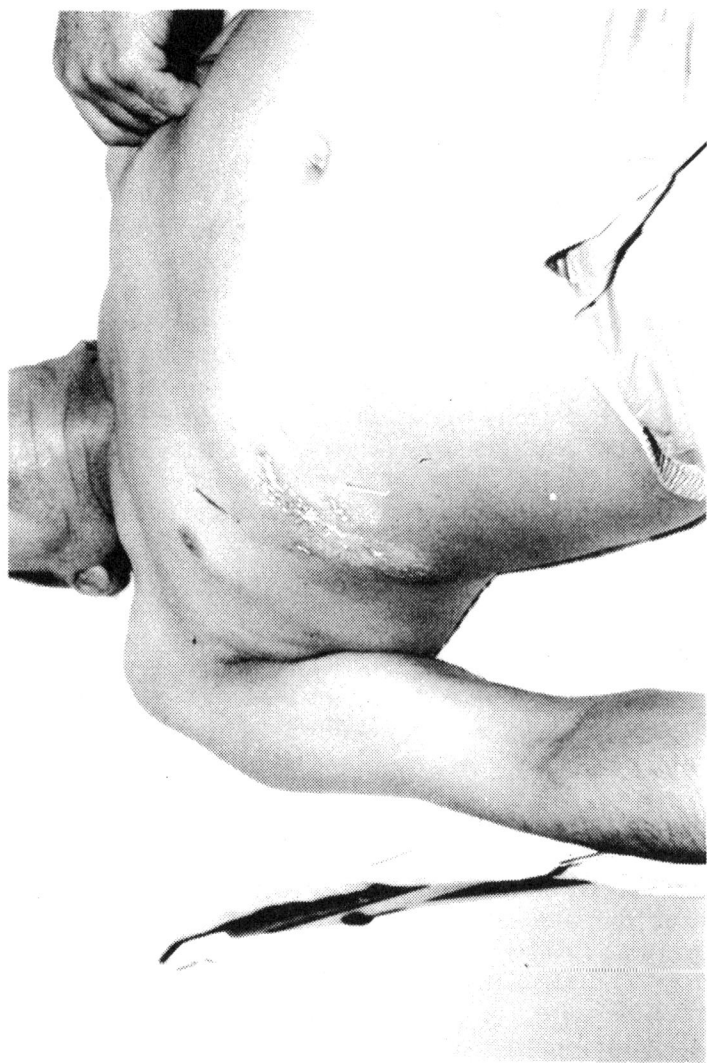

The treatment of shingles using body acupuncture.

cent of cases of trigeminal neuralgia. Judging by the experience of Western acupuncturists this success rate represents a rather high figure, although acupuncture can undoubtedly have a beneficial effect on this type of pain.

Postherpetic neuralgia is the pain that occurs after an attack of shingles. Shingles is a viral infection of the nerves, and the nerves affected by shingles can occasionally continue to cause severe pain after the shingles has cleared.

Postherpetic neuralgia is an uncommon disease in China; this may be because the Chinese treat all cases of shingles with acupuncture before the postherpetic neuralgia can develop. There are other possible explanations for its decreased incidence in China, perhaps postherpetic neuralgia is affected by diet, or racial characteristics; however, it is much more reasonable to suggest that the dearth of postherpetic neuralgia in China is due to the daily treatment of shingles with acupuncture. It seems that of those patients with established postherpetic neuralgia, about 40 per cent gain some degree of long term benefit from acupuncture. If this figure could be substantiated with proper clinical research work, it would represent a significant advance in the treatment of this condition.

There are a vast number of aches and pains that are often described as neuralgic. Many of these occur as facial pain and most of them cause severe discomfort. It is always worth while to attempt to alleviate these pains by using acupuncture. Some people respond and others do not; it is impossible to give figures for success, or even estimates, without going into great detail about the exact cause and type of neuralgia being treated.

Anxiety, Depression and Other Nervous Disorders

It is difficult to be objective about the treatment of disorders such as anxiety and depression, as the problems themselves are difficult to assess objectively, and therefore no good clear figures are available about their treatment with acupuncture.

In spite of this, many acupuncturists, including the Chinese, treat a wide range of 'mental disorders' with acupuncture. Many people have stated that acupuncture is clearly effective in helping symptoms such as insomnia and bed-wetting, and can also create a feeling of general well-being. Patients who receive acupuncture for specific problems, such as ankle pain, will often note how well they feel after the treatment. It would be very misleading to give figures of 'cure rates' for these problems because such disorders naturally relapse and remit, often improving when a sympathetic listener becomes involved. I think it is fair to say, however, that acupuncture can sometimes effect mood changes that help these problems significantly.

The Chinese have completed trials on some of the more clearly defined and serious mental diseases, such as schizophrenia. In a trial involving over 400 patients they claim a 54 per cent cure rate for this disease, with a further 30 per cent showing 'significant improvement'. These figures are exceptionally high and, if correct, are most interesting. Their criteria for evaluating a 'cure' or a 'significant improvement' are not clearly stated and so it is difficult to be sure whether these results are valid. Many claims have been made for the effects of acupuncture in the treatment of a variety of 'nervous disorders' but, sadly, there is no good hard evidence to substantiate or refute such claims; however, from a variety of excellent research papers it is clear that acupuncture can influence quite radically many areas of the central nervous system. This work is of a purely scientific nature and at present it is not directly applicable to the clinical effects of acupuncture therapy.

Nerve Paralysis

There are three major types of nerve destruction that cause paralysis. Children may be born with an incomplete nervous system, such as spina bifida, an accident may occur that destroys part of the nervous system, or a disease may be present causing destruction or disfunction of nervous tissue.

Chinese research workers claim that acupuncture can be used to treat the symptoms of spina bifida, such as incontinence, although no claim has been made that acupuncture can affect the anatomical abnormality.

Traumatic paralysis, due to accidental destruction of the nervous system, can also be treated by a variety of acupuncture techniques. The acupuncture must be continued for a long period, sometimes daily for six months, but the results from some of the Chinese work are encouraging. They claim that some 50-60 per cent of patients are likely to gain significant return of function if treated with acupuncture, but it is wise to remember that a good number of these injuries would allow the spontaneous recovery of significant function.

Facial paralysis (Bell's palsy) is a disease of sudden onset that causes one side of the face to lose muscular power; the cause of this is unknown. Acupuncture and moxibustion can be used to treat this and the Chinese claim a 75 per cent complete recovery rate but, again, this disease allows a significant percentage of spontaneous recovery. The Chinese also claim that a further 20 per cent gain benefit from acupuncture, although not complete recovery. Even allowing for the known level of spontaneous resolution in facial paralysis it does seem that acupuncture has something extra to offer.

Other Nervous Diseases

Acupuncture has been claimed to be effective in Parkinson's disease, nerve deafness, and a large variety of other problems. Some of these claims are far from proven (or disproven), but it is always wise to remember that acupuncture is a harmless technique and can sometimes give excellent results where other medical methods have failed.

DISEASES OF THE DIGESTIVE SYSTEM

There has not been a great deal of good clinical research work published about the effects of acupuncture on the digestive system, so it is difficult to be sure exactly how useful it is in such diseases. This section is therefore deliberately rather vague as it is far more sensible not to quote exact facts and figures when there is little evidence to substantiate them. Animal experiments, both in China and the West, show quite clearly that acupuncture does have an effect on the digestive system, and in spite of the lack of clinical research there are good grounds for believing that acupuncture can influence a variety of disorders within this system.

Indigestion

Indigestion is a symptom rather than a disease, and can be caused by a variety of factors such as over-indulgence, stress and acid regurgitation. It is important to investigate long-standing indigestion so that the exact reasons for this symptom can be clearly defined.

Acid regurgitation is one of the commoner causes of indigestion and often presents with symptoms such as heartburn. The sensation of heartburn is caused by irritation due to the acid reflux from the stomach into the tube connecting the stomach to the mouth (the oesophagus). This syndrome may be called a 'hiatus hernia' although a variety of other names can also be used to describe exactly the same symptoms.

Acupuncture is not the treatment of choice for all types of indigestion. For instance, the best treatment for over-indulgence is to eat less, but some other causes of indigestion such as hiatus hernia and stress are definitely amenable to acupuncture therapy. Exact figures for success rates are not available, but the 'clinical impression' that arises from a number of acupuncturists indicates that about 60 per cent of patients gain some long-term relief of their symptoms with acupuncture. Symptoms do recur and usually require re-treatment after about six to twelve months.

Stomach Ulcers

An ulcer is an area of raw tissue, rather like the tissue found under the scab of a healing cut. Ulcers can occur in the stomach and are usually found either in the stomach proper (gastric ulcers), or in the part of the intestine that drains food from the stomach (duodenal ulcers). Stomach ulcers are a common problem but their exact cause is unknown.

In China acupuncture is the treatment of choice for stomach ulcers, and ulcers certainly do heal after acupuncture. Fortunately both types of stomach ulcer heal spontaneously and this creates a great deal of difficulty in assessing the curative effects of acupuncture as compared to natural remission; furthermore, there are now available some highly effective and relatively non-toxic drugs to cure ulcers.

Duodenal ulcers are associated with a high acid level in the stomach. It is unclear exactly how much this factor affects the development of duodenal ulcers, but it is fair to say that high acid levels are a factor in ulcer development. Research work by Chinese physiologists has shown, quite clearly, that acupuncture can reduce the acidity of the stomach and this may be one of

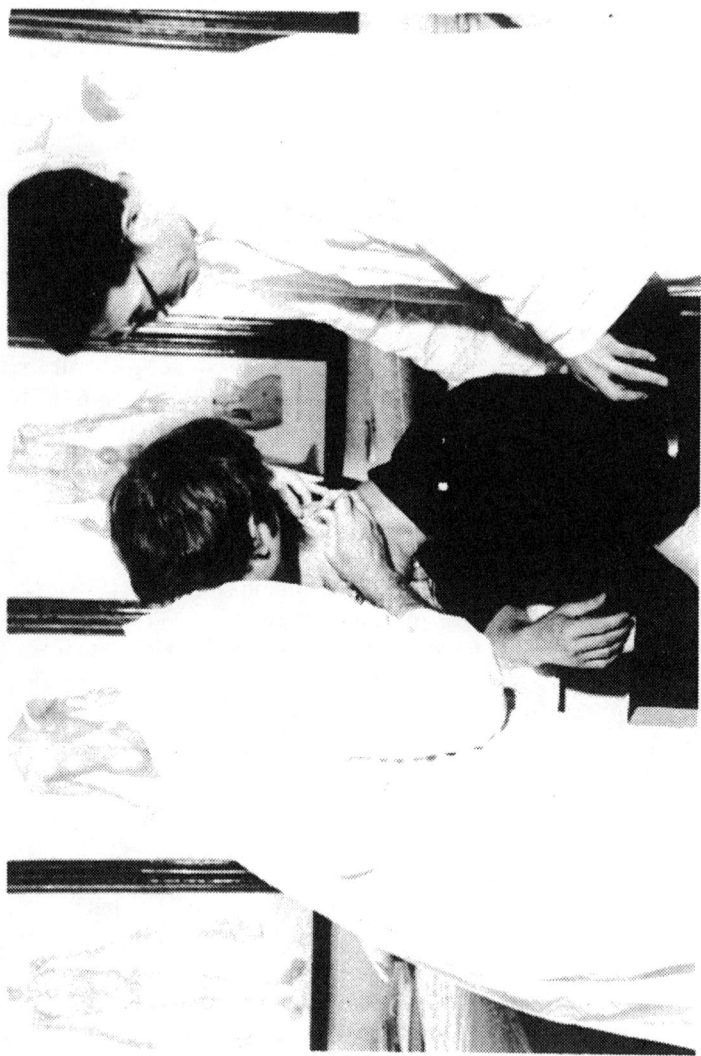

Probing the ear in order to select an effective acupuncture point.

the mechanisms by which acupuncture heals stomach ulcers and other digestive diseases.

Gall Stones

A large volume of work has been published by the Chinese about the effects of acupuncture on the gall bladder. It would seem that acupuncture can cause the discharge of quite large gall stones in the faeces, obviating the necessity for most operations to remove the gall bladder. The Chinese studies are of great interest but it is too soon to draw valid long-term conclusions about this work.

Diarrhoea

Diarrhoea is a symptom that can be indicative of a variety of diseases; it may be caused by an infection (dysentery), an inflammatory process (colitis), stress or dietary indiscretion. Sometimes no clear cause can be found for irregular bowel habits and these ill-defined problems are usually called 'irritable bowel syndrome'.

Studies on bowel infections, completed in China, show that acupuncture affects the natural history of this disease. The Chinese report that recovery is quicker, and complications less frequent, if acupuncture is given in this condition. Clear evidence is also provided to show that acupuncture 'improves' the natural defences of the body in these types of infection. A large body of evidence is now available, showing that acupuncture stimulates the body's natural defences in many infectious diseases; this again suggests another possible mechanism for the effects of acupuncture. Acupuncture can be shown to alter the activity of the immuno system, stimulating the production of immunoglobulins (chemicals that help to kill invading bacteria), and various other important substances. This measurable effect lends support to the philosophical idea that acupuncture helps the body to cure disease naturally.

Diseases such as Crohn's disease, ulcerative colitis and colitis are collectively described as inflammatory bowel diseases. The exact cause of these problems is unknown. When inflammatory bowel disease is present the intestines become raw and inflamed and the patient usually complains of symptoms such as abdominal pain, blood loss and diarrhoea. These diseases are often difficult to treat with the available Western therapeutics, but they are sometimes amenable to acupuncture. Exact figures describing success rates are not available at present.

Irritable bowel syndrome and diarrhoea caused by stress can also be improved by acupuncture, but clear facts and figures are not available and further research is required in this field.

Piles

Piles are a common cause of human misery; they are really varicose veins occurring around the anus and rectum. Once again no clear figures are available about cure rates, but piles are said to be helped by acupuncture.

DISEASES OF THE RESPIRATORY SYSTEM

Asthma

The wheeze of asthma is caused by contraction of the muscular walls of the small breathing tubes in the lung. The narrowed air tube creates a 'turbulent' air flow and therefore causes a wheeze, or whistle, when the asthmatic breathes. Because the tubes into the lung are narrowed, less air can get in and this decreases the oxygen supply to the body. The muscular contraction of the breathing tubes can be stimulated by a wide range of substances such as inhaled dust or pollen, and various foods.

Acupuncture causes the contracted muscular walls to dilate; the mechanism of this is unknown, but there is good Western research data to support this claim. A recent Chinese clinical trial on asthma showed that some 70 per cent of asthmatics gained a 'good effect' from a course of acupuncture and moxibustion (about ten treatments) once a year. The acupuncture treatment was able to decrease the frequency and intensity of asthmatic attacks over a period of a year. This result is encouraging as it shows that acupuncture and moxibustion can affect the response of the body to the environmental stimuli causing asthmatic attacks.

Bronchitis

Bronchitis is a common lung disease, aggravated by cigarette smoke, industrial pollutants, and dust. It involves the irreparable destruction of lung tissue. There is often an asthmatic element in bronchitis as irritants such as smoke and dust cause the muscular walls of the breathing tubes to contract.

Acupuncture cannot rebuild lung tissue, but by opening up the breathing tubes it can allow the remaining lung tissue to function efficiently. The mechanism of acupuncture in bronchitis is probably much the same as in asthma, allowing more air to enter the lungs. Recent Chinese work has shown that about 50 per cent of bronchitics 'benefit' from acupuncture. The treatment must be repeated regularly if the effect is to be maintained.

DISEASES OF THE HEART AND BLOOD VESSELS

In the West, diseases of the circulatory system are not commonly treated with acupuncture, but in China it is a common and acceptable form of treatment for some of these problems. A variety of animal experiments carried out in the West give clear support to the idea that acupuncture does have an effect on the circulatory system.

Angina
Angina is a type of 'cramp' in the heart muscles, precipitated by a poor blood supply to the heart, and it usually exhibits itself as chest pain on exercise. Using sophisticated measuring equipment the Chinese have completed a variety of trials to assess the effects of acupuncture on the heart, and they have shown a marked increase in the functional ability and efficiency of the heart muscles after acupuncture.

This is further supported by clinical work, which shows that some 80 per cent of patients with angina have improved after acupuncture. When acupuncture is used to treat angina a course of treatments is given, and then followed by booster treatments every four to six months.

The Correction of Abnormal Heart Rhythms
Heart diseases can frequently cause an abnormal rhythm to the heart beat; this may manifest itself as palpitations, an irregular heart beat, or dropped beats. Acupuncture can correct a small

number of these arrhythmias. In established atrial fibrillation (irregular heart beats), acupuncture affects a small percentage of cases, some 1.5 per cent, although in recently acquired arrhythmias, acupuncture can be effective in up to 70 per cent of cases.

Raised Blood Pressure

Traditional Chinese medicine does not recognize raised blood pressure (hypertension) as a disease, and acupuncture treatment has therefore centred around the relief of the infrequent and vague symptoms associated with raised blood pressure, such as headaches and dizziness. In Western medical circles there is great debate about whether raised blood pressure should be treated as aggressively as it has been in the past. Acupuncture and moxibustion can lower the blood pressure, but there is no good work available to show how useful this is on a long or short term basis. At present, the whole concept of raised blood pressure and its treatment is unclear, and the place of acupuncture in the treatment of this problem is unknown.

THE USE OF ACUPUNCTURE IN ADDICTION AND OBESITY

A large number of Western acupuncturists are using a variety of acupuncture techniques to treat obesity, smoking and hard drug addiction. There is some excellent physiological and clinical evidence to support the use of acupuncture in these areas. The withdrawal symptoms experienced by people giving up smoking, or drugs, can be alleviated by raising the levels of endorphins in the nervous system.[1] Some people believe that the desire to eat is also mediated by the endorphin level in the brain. It is clear that endorphin levels throughout the nervous system can be increased by acupuncture. The techniques used to achieve an increase in endorphin levels centre around the use of ear acupuncture; the ear may be electrically stimulated or a small staple or stud may be left in the ear for a week at a time. Pressing the indwelling needle seems to decrease the desire to smoke or eat, probably due to an increase in the endorphin level.

---

[1] The effect of acupuncture on endorphin levels is discussed in Chapter 3.

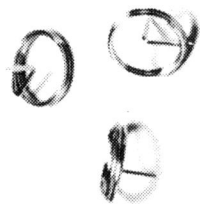

Press studs used for ear acupuncture. These studs may remain in the ear for about a week.

It must be stressed that acupuncture cannot replace will-power. It can only help the withdrawal symptoms, or hunger pains, experienced by those already motivated and committed to solving their particular problem.

Obesity

Acupuncture seems to relieve the problem of hunger usually created by dieting. Many people who receive acupuncture to help with weight loss also go on a diet at the same time. It is difficult to assess exactly which factors are responsible for weight loss, the acupuncture or the diet, or both in combination. Most acupuncturists claim that 40-50 per cent of their patients experience some significant weight loss (about ten pounds) during treatment. The figures are vague as no useful trials have been completed in this field. It seems that ear acupuncture can help to suppress hunger, but it is unlikely to affect greed!

Hard Drug Addiction

Some excellent research work has been done in this field, especially in Hong Kong. It is clear that acupuncture can help to solve the severe withdrawal symptoms experienced by those coming off hard drugs like heroin; however, withdrawal from drugs is only half the battle as a proper programme of rehabilitation is required if hard drug addicts are to return to the community, and acupuncture can only provide assistance in part of this battle.

Smoking

It is claimed that ear acupuncture helps about 40 per cent of people to give up smoking over a period of about six months. Again, it is essential to be well motivated before embarking on a course of treatment. Acupuncture does seem to decrease the desire to smoke and also to alleviate the withdrawal symptoms produced by abstinence from tobacco.

Acupuncture does have an effect on addictions and obesity, although the effect is limited and some of the claims made for acupuncture in this field may be due to other associated factors.

THE USE OF ACUPUNCTURE IN OBSTETRICS

In China the major use of acupuncture in obstetrics is to provide analgesia (pain relief) during Caesarean section, and to correct foetal malpositions, such as breech (breech means when the baby is 'bottom first' rather than 'head first').

Foetal Malposition
The correction of foetal malposition is achieved by applying moxibustion to an acupuncture point on the little toe. In about 60 per cent of women the foetus turns naturally prior to the thirty-fourth week of pregnancy; this can be increased to 90 per cent with the aid of moxibustion. After the thirty-fourth week, when natural version is less likely, the Chinese claim that 80 per cent of foetal malpositions will be corrected permanently by this procedure. Once corrected, the malposition does not recur, provided moxibustion is applied daily. There seems to be no available physiological basis with which to explain this finding.

Anaesthesia for Labour and Delivery
Acupuncture anaesthesia is widely used for Caesarean sections in China. A report recently published by the Chinese, discusses the results of 1,000 cases managed in this manner. The Chinese claim a 98 per cent success rate in the abolition of pain, a quicker recovery rate from the operation, less blood loss, and the obvious advantage of the mother being able to see the baby at, or soon after, birth. This report finds acupuncture a superior form of analgesia compared to other forms of pain relief (general or epidural anaesthesia) for Caesarean section. This success rate is astonishingly high and may well be a rather 'enthusiastic' claim.

Acupuncture can also be used to provide pain relief in normal obstetric deliveries. Adequate assessment of this form of obstetric analgesia has not yet been published, although the experience of a wide variety of acupuncturists in the West would indicate that it is a useful and effective procedure.

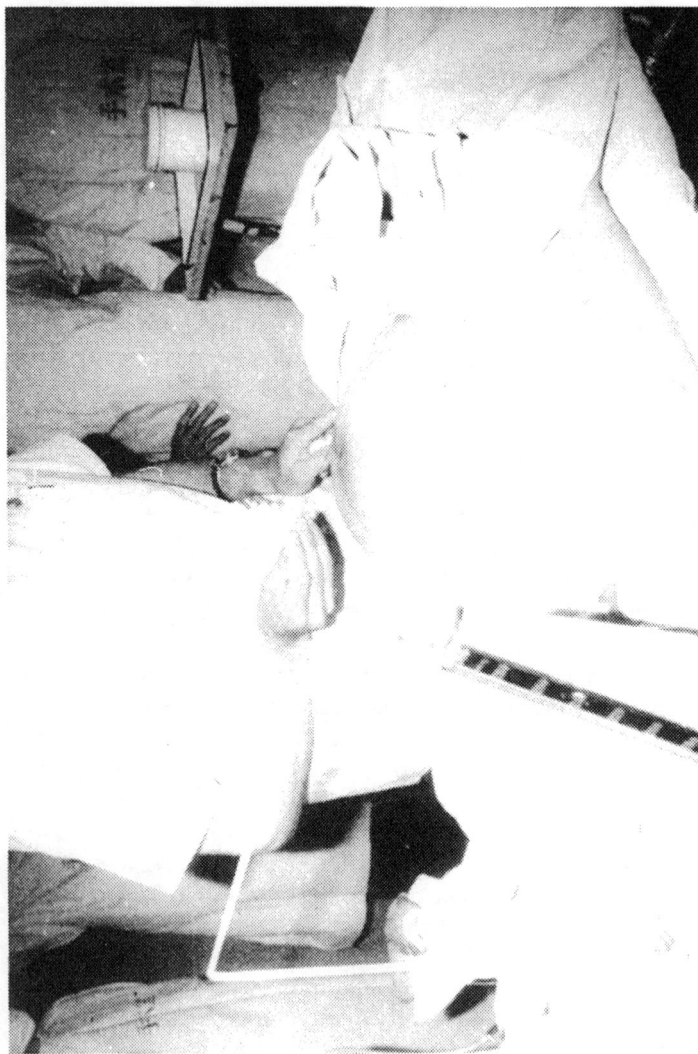

Needle insertion for a Caesarean section under acupuncture analgesia.

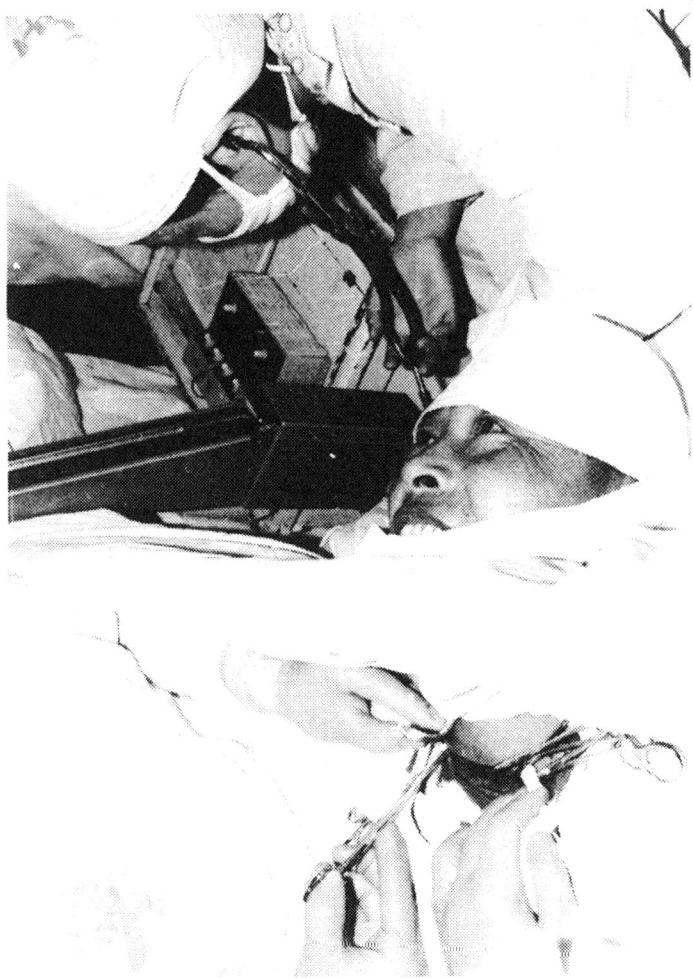

A thyroid operation using acupuncture analgesia.

ACUPUNCTURE ANAESTHESIA

Acupuncture anaesthesia is widely used in China. It often provides the highlight to a 'tourist trip' and has been filmed for the Western media on many occasions. Acupuncture anaesthesia has been used in a wide variety of operations, from minor procedures to open heart surgery. It is undoubtedly an effective form of pain relief in the majority of people, but there is always a small percentage who fail to gain adequate analgesia from acupuncture. These failures are quoted at between one and twenty per cent, depending on the operation and the assessments used.

In general, acupuncture allows for a safer operation, with less likelihood of complications, and a swifter post-operative recovery. The main problem is that pain relief may be inadequate and this is unacceptable within the context of Western health care.

One of the main criticisms of acupuncture anaesthesia is that 'it's alright for the Chinese, but won't work on Europeans'. Acupuncture anaesthesia has been used in a variety of European centres, and the success and failure rate is much the same as in China. Acupuncture anaesthesia is a useful method of pain relief and could well be applicable to minor procedures, or post-operative pain relief, within the context of a Western medical system.

6. The History of Acupuncture in China

Acupuncture, or needle puncture, is a European term invented by Willem Ten Rhyne, a Dutch physician who visited Nagasaki in Japan in the early part of the seventeenth century. The Chinese describe acupuncture by the character 'Chen', which literally means 'to prick with a needle', a graphic description of this therapeutic technique.

Early History

Acupuncture has a clearly recorded history of about 2,000 years, but some authorities claim that it has been practised in China for some 4,000 years. The Chinese believe that the practice of acupuncture began during the Stone Age when stone knives or sharp edged tools, described by the character 'Bian', were used to puncture and drain abcesses. In fact the Chinese character 'Bian' means the 'use of a sharp edged stone to treat disease', and the modern Chinese character 'Bi', representing a disease of pain, is almost certainly derived from the use of 'Bian stones' for the treatment of painful complaints.

The origin of Chinese medicine is a fascinating story and acupuncture represents only one facet of their medical system. The first recorded attempt at conceptualizing and treating disease dates back to about 1500 B.C. during the Shang dynasty. Tortoise shells with inscriptions dating from that time have been found, and it is thought that these were used for divination in the art of healing. The philosophical basis of much of the very early

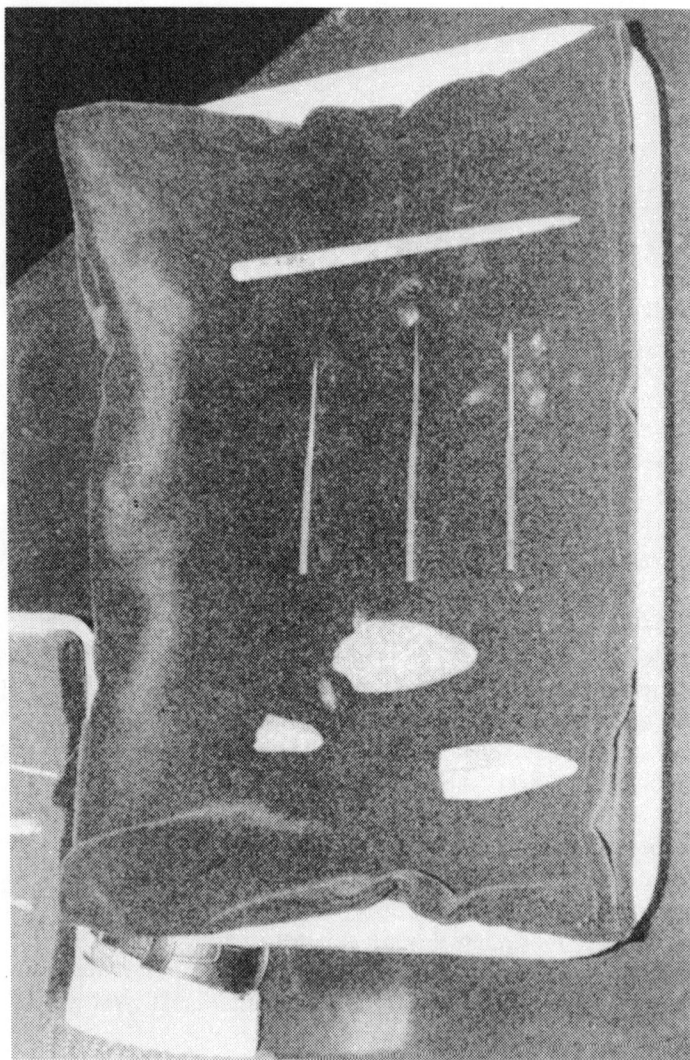

Early stone and bone acupuncture needles (Bian stones).

Chinese medicine seems to have been to seek harmony between the living and their dead ancestors, and the good and evil spirits that inhabited the earth.

The Development of the Chinese Approach
to Medicine and Science

The first known acupuncture text is the *Nei Ching Su Wen* and there is a great deal of controversy about the exact origins and authorship of this book. The *Nei Ching Su Wen* is divided into two main sections, the *Su Wen*, or simple questions and the *Ling Shu*, or difficult questions. The book is also known by a variety of alternative titles such as the *Yellow Emperor's Classic of Internal Medicine*, or the *Canon of Medicine*, but all these titles refer to the same basic text.

The initial section of the *Nei Ching Su Wen* involves a discussion between the Yellow Emperor, Huang Ti, and his Minister, Ch'i Pai. This discussion lays down the philosophical basis of traditional Chinese medicine, and makes the *Nei Ching Su Wen* more of a treatise on health and disease rather than a textbook of medicine. Early Greek texts on medicine are mainly of interest to the medical historian rather than the practising physician. For instance, Hippocrates does make many excellent philosophical and practical observations about disease and the doctor-patient relationship, but for the most part these texts are recipe books for a variety of ill-defined diseases. The *Nei Ching Su Wen* is timeless and deals almost exclusively with philosophical concepts, many of which seem to be as important today as they were 2,000 years ago.

Professor Joseph Needham, one of the greatest living experts on Chinese scientific philosophy, describes some aspects of the ancient Chinese system of science as mediaeval and retrogressive. He feels that many of these concepts have distorted that development and obvious potential of Chinese medicine. There is undoubtedly an element of truth in this but there is still a great deal of useful and valuable information within the traditional Chinese approach to medicine.

The Western doctor observes the facts before him and uses the current physiological theories to explain them. Chinese medicine is based on a much wider world view, which is described in the *Nei Ching Su Wen*, and these ideas are woven into a complete and intact system based on a philosophy different from that of modern Western medicine. The concepts of Yin and Yang, and the number five, are two of the more important ideas that permeate much of traditional Chinese scientific thought.

Yin and Yang are opposite aspects of the material world. Like night and day they are interdependent, and the existence of one end of the spectrum presupposes the existence of the other aspect; i.e. Yin is necessary for Yang to exist, and vice versa. At first the idea of Yin and Yang seems very simplistic; it is not, it describes the fundamental fluctuating balance of nature. A modern concept that pre-supposes the existence of Yin and Yang is ecology, one of the main principles of which is that the forces of the environment must be in a fluctuating balance.

The number five is also very important to Chinese thought. For example, there are five notes in the musical scale, five tastes for food and five elements in the physical world (earth, fire, water, wood and metal). The five elements are not just the atomic constituents of matter, they have also been described as the five transitional stages of all physical materials. It is these philosophical ideas that form the basis of much of the discussion in the *Nei Ching Su Wen*.

The authorship of the *Nei Ching Su Wen* is attributed to Huang Ti, the Yellow Emperor, but there is some doubt as to whether Huang Ti actually existed and a great deal more doubt about the claim that he wrote the *Nei Ching Su Wen*. Genealogies of the Chinese dynasties list him as the third of the first five rulers of China, and ascribe the dates 2697-2579 B.C. to him. Ssu-Ma Ch'ien, an historian of the second century B.C., begins the *Historical Records* with an account of Huang Ti and defines him as the founder of the Chinese civilization, and the first ruler of the Empire. He is one of three legendary Emperors who founded the art of healing; the others are Shen Nung and Fu Hsi.

It is probable that the *Nei Ching Su Wen* was written by a variety of people and was updated by several important Chinese physicians. Some authorities date the *Nei Ching Su Wen* from 1000 B.C. whilst others, probably more correctly, date this text to the Warring States period (475-221 B.C.). The *Ling Shu* was almost certainly added during the Warring States period, and

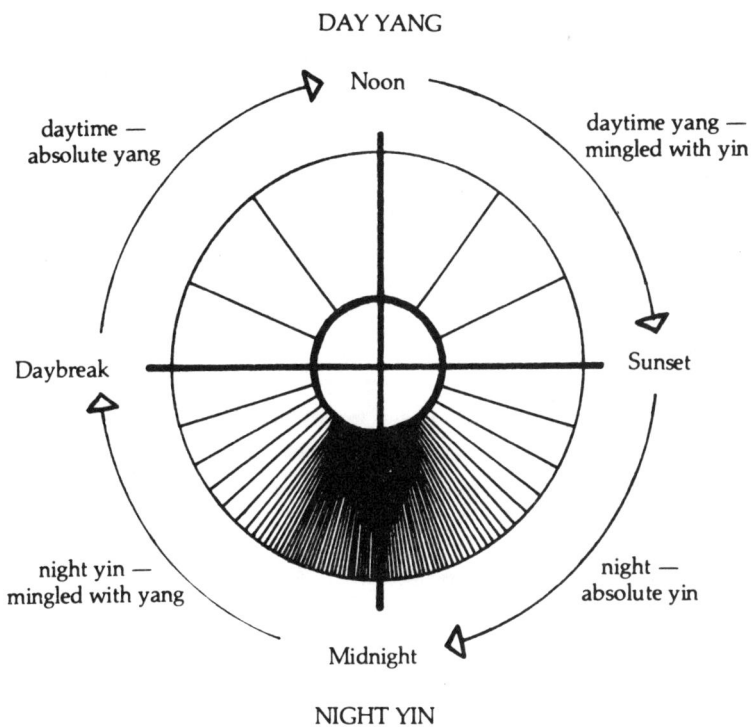

The ever-changing balance of Yin and Yang, illustrated by the cycle of day and night.

the twenty-four chapters that comprise the *Nei Ching Su Wen*
were probably revised and re-written at this time.

The Development of Chinese Philosophy

The Warring States period is a particularly interesting time in
Chinese history and has exerted a great deal of influence on
Chinese thought. Two main philosophical ideologies became
part of the mainstream of Chinese thought at this time, Taoism
and Confucianism.

Confucianism defined the social status of prince and pauper
within Chinese society and elected the Emperor a god. It resulted
in a basically feudal and totalitarian system of government that
still exists today, in an adapted form. Confucianism impinged
on medicine in that it was opposed to the development of
anatomy and surgery, one of its main tenets being that the whole
body was sacred and should remain complete throughout life,
and also in death. The Confucians believed that it was
important to present oneself to 'the ancestors' whole, and therefore one of the most feared methods of execution in ancient
China was decapitation. Acupuncture and related methods
were the logical answer to this constraint, as they were able to
cure internal disease with external means.

The Tao literally means the 'way' and the philosophy of
Taoism is a method of maintaining harmony between man and
his world, and between this world and beyond. The Tao, or the
'way', has been linked to a separate creed called Taoism but its
basic naturalistic philosophies permeate all Chinese thought and
religion, including Buddhism. Yin and Yang are very much part
of the Tao, as the *Book of Changes* states, 'one Yin, one Yang,
being called the Tao'. The religion of Taoism became formalized
during the Warring States period and a book of poems entitled
the *Tao* attributed to Lao Tsu (c. 500 B.C.), describes many of the
basic concepts within this philosophy.

The Taoist concept of health is to attempt to attain perfect
harmony between the opposing forces of the natural world,
between Yin and Yang, the belief being that the only way to be
healthy is to adjust to the natural forces within the world and to
become part of their rhythm. It is further realized that these
natural forces are completely dependent on each other; earth is
dependent on rain and rain is dependent on heaven, which in

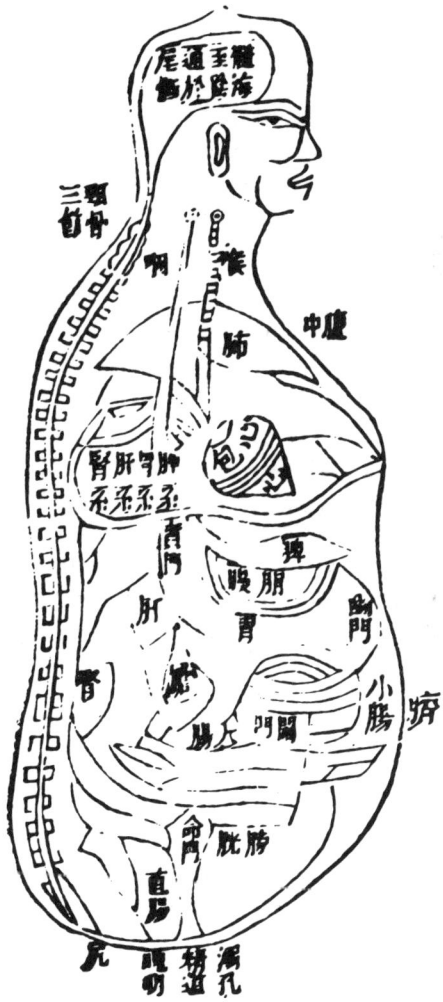

新改正內景之圖

心系七節七節之傍中有小心以
腎系十四椎下由下而上亦七節

舊圖有精道循脊背過肛門且無
子宮命門之象皆誤也今改正之

尾通主
閭腎脊髓海

顋骨
三節

咽

嚨

肺

中膲

腎肝氣肛
系系系

膈

青門

脾

胃

朋

幽門

肝

小腸 痹

腸大

闌門

腎

命門 肫膀

直腸

尾

穀道 精孔
肛門

The Internal organs, from 'I Tsung Pi Tu' compiled about A.D. 1575.

turn cannot exist without the earth. In the same way Yin cannot exist without Yang, and yet the two are opposites. The concept of a unified, but at the same time polar force, governing natural events, is central to much of Chinese thought.

At first glance these concepts seem to be an irrelevant side-line to the development of a system of medicine, but acupuncture and its development can only really be understood if the reader grasps the traditional Chinese approach to health and disease. In essence, the ideal of health is perfect harmony between the forces of Yin and Yang; this represents the correct 'way' or the Tao. Disharmony brings disease and death. Taoism is a passive philosophy, exalting the art of detailed and accurate observation. This was also an essential part of the development of Chinese medical thought and allowed detailed observations on organ structure and function to be made, as discussed in the first chapter.

Acupuncture Needles

As acupuncture developed, the Bian stones were discarded and needles of stone and pottery were used. These simple, primitive needles are still used in some of the rural areas of China. Eventually metal needles began to appear and these took the form of the classical 'nine needles'. The 'nine needles' comprised the arrowhead needle for superficial pricking, the round needle for massaging, the blunt needle for knocking or pressing, the three-edged needle for puncturing a vein, the sword-like needle for draining abcesses, the sharp round needle for rapid pricking, the filliform needle, the long needle for thick muscles and the large needle for puncturing painful joints.

The main needle now used for acupuncture is the filliform as most of the others have been replaced by more sophisticated surgical instruments, for instance, the sword-like needle has been replaced by the scalpel.

The 'nine needles' were initially made of either bronze, or gold and silver, and seem to have been first used about 2,000 years ago. The tomb of the Prince of Chungshan, dating from the second century B.C., was excavated in 1968 and contained a set of nine needles, four being of gold and five of silver. Some acupuncturists use gold and silver needles but the majority use only stainless steel filliform needles.

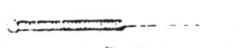

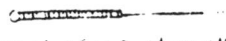

The original nine needles from 'Zhen Jiu Du Cheng' compiled in 1601.

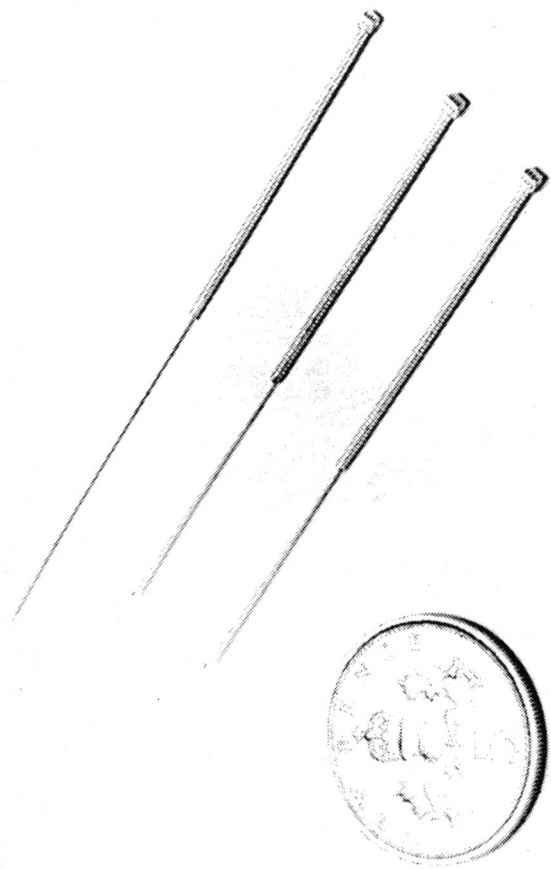

One and one and a half inch acupuncture needles compared with a 5p coin.

Moxibustion

A discussion of the history of acupuncture is incomplete without mentioning moxibustion. Moxibustion is the burning on the skin of the herb moxa. The Chinese character 'Chiu' is used to describe the art of moxibustion, and literally means 'to scar with a burning object'. Moxibustion does not now involve scarring, but moxa is still used to provide local heat over acupuncture points. It is made from the dried leaves of *Artemisia vulgaris* and the Chinese believe that the older the moxa, the better its therapeutic properties.

Moxibustion developed as a medical practice completely separate from acupuncture, although it is now very much a part of current acupuncture practice in China. It is used to treat specific types of disease and is applied over the same body points (acupuncture points) as acupuncture needles. Some of the acupuncture points, such as those around the eye, are forbidden to moxa. In ancient China, moxa was also burnt on specific acupuncture points to keep the body healthy, and was said to act as a prophylactic against disease.

Moxa can be used in a variety of ways. Loose moxa is made into a cone and burnt on the skin, the cone then being removed when it is half burnt, to avoid blistering. It may also be burnt on ginger or garlic so that the skin is isolated from extreme heat, or a moxa stick may be used and burnt a centimetre or two away from the skin.

Initial Therapeutic Success

The exceptionally productive period of the Warring States also gives us the first known and recorded therapeutic success of acupuncture. The *Historical Records* by Ssu-ma Ch'ien tells how the physician Pien Cheuh used acupuncture to revive the Governor of the State of Kuo from a coma. In fact the name of the physician was Chin Yeuh-jen, but by taking the legendary name of the famous Chinese physician, Pein Cheuh, we can assess his prestige. The Governor was treated by acupuncture and subsequently with herbal medicines. In ancient China, as today, an event like this is a powerful argument in favour of the acceptance of any form of treatment.

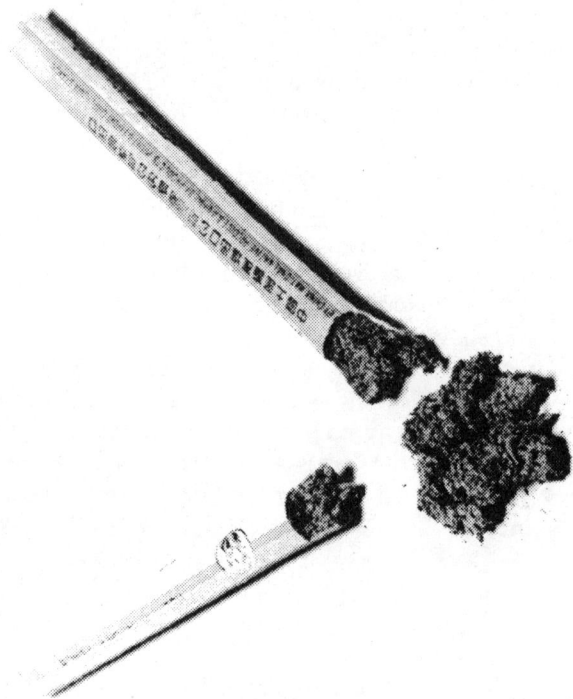

Moxa rolls with loose moxa.

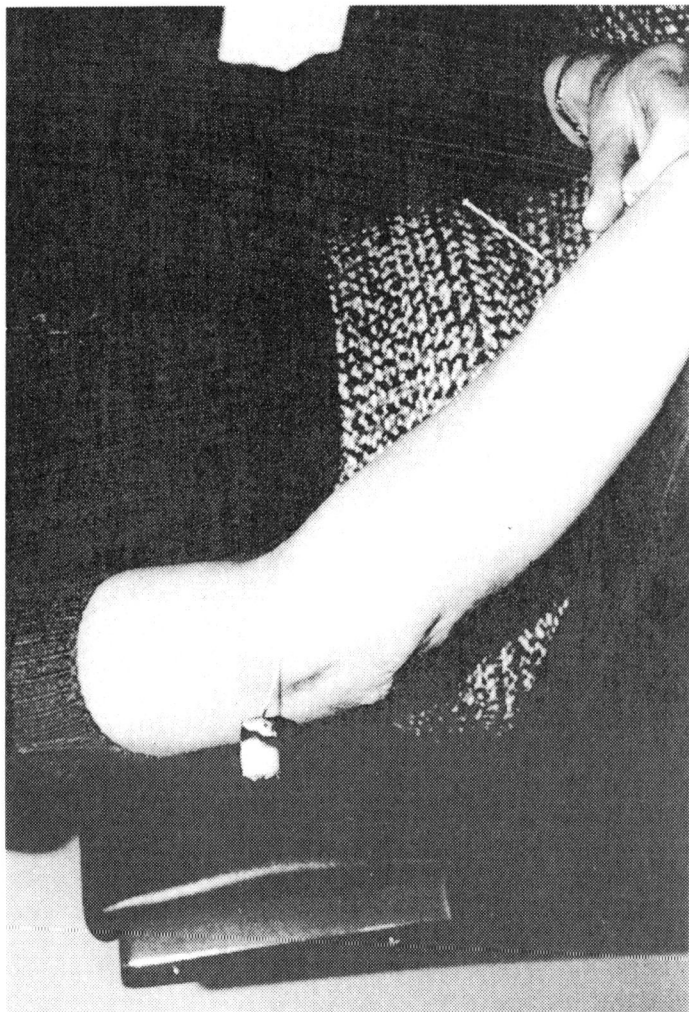

Moxa applied to a needle for the treatment of tennis elbow (warm needling).

The Evolution of Acupuncture Points and Channels

Initially, there were no specific locations on the body for applying either moxa or acupuncture but gradually, through empirical experience, the use of specific points on the skin were shown to be of value in particular diseases. Acupuncture points are undoubtedly the end-product of millions of detailed observations and as they were developed so each of them was given a name and Chinese character, depending on its therapeutic properties.

Acupuncture points were subsequently grouped into a system of channels which run over the body, conducting the flow of vital energy through the body. The acupuncture points on a channel are said to influence the flow of vital energy through the channel, thereby influencing disease processes in the body. The first clear reference to the points and channels is in the *Nei Ching Su Wen* which defines the main channels and acupuncture points. The *Nei Ching Su Wen* also makes the observation 'in pain, puncture the tender spot', and the use of painful points probably represents the original method by which many of the acupuncture points were discovered. There is an instinctive urge to cause more pain over a painful area; the image of a person with toothache, pressing on the painful tooth, is a frequent cartoonists' joke. Common painful diseases consistently cause painful points to emerge in well defined anatomical locations over the body. When this point is stimulated the pain can be alleviated; hence the idea of a point for treating pain. From this simple beginning it is easy to see how a system of acupuncture points evolved.

The evolution of the channels connecting these acupuncture points is more difficult to understand. These seem to have evolved from an intuitive understanding of the flow of vital energy through the body. It is unclear from where the idea of the channels originated, but for the last 2,000 years they have formed an essential part of traditional Chinese medicine.

Acupuncture Texts and Teaching Methods

Another major text, the *Classic of Acupuncture and Moxibustion*, also made its appearance during the Warring States period. This was written by Huang Fu Mi in the third century B.C. Together with the *Nei Ching Su Wen* these two texts form

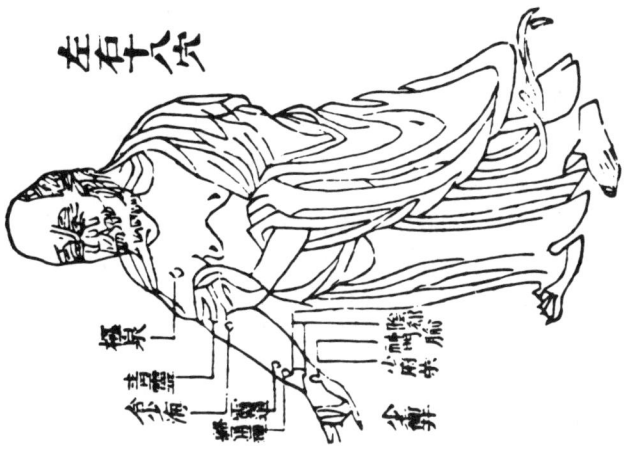

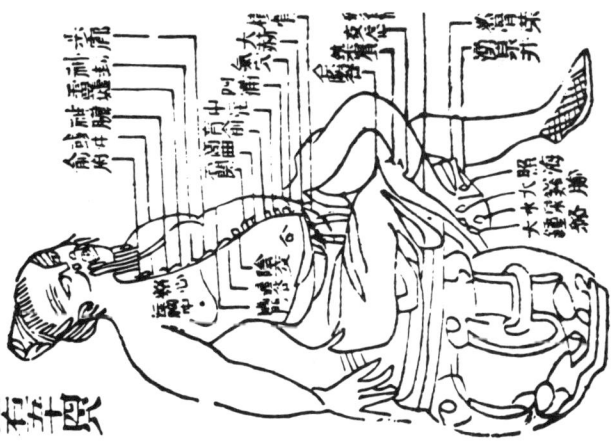

The heart and kidney channels from 'Ling Shu Su Wen Chieh Yao'.

the basis for the anatomical descriptions of the main channels, and some 349 acupuncture points on these channels. The Warring States period saw the coalescence of acupuncture, and indeed most of Chinese thought, in the mould in which it existed until the recent Communist revolution.

During the Sui dynasty (A.D. 561-618) the first medical college in China was founded. The Imperial Medical College was established to administer medical research and to train doctors. Acupuncture and moxibustion, as well as herbal medicine, formed the basis of the curriculum. According to the *Old History of the Tang Dynasty* the Imperial College had one professor of acupuncture, ten instructors, twenty needle craftsmen and twenty students. The main teaching texts were the *Nei Ching Su Wen* and the *Classic of Acupuncture and Moxibustion*. The bulk of the teaching and practice of traditional Chinese medicine, however, has never been based in formalized medical colleges, although these colleges have been in existence since the Sui dynasty. The medical arts have more often been handed down from father to son, or from master to apprentice. This type of medical apprenticeship has only recently died out, and in fact some of the older acupuncturists in China today have been trained in this way.

The Tang dynasty saw a great flowering of the art of acupuncture, and the *Thousand Golden Remedies* by Sun Szu-Miao was one of the products of this period. This text was the first to contain clear colour charts of the channels with front, side and back views of the body; obviously a great boon to students and teachers of acupuncture. We are aware of the existence of these charts from the references made to them in a number of other texts, but unfortunately they have been lost.

Printing and Language
China developed the art of printing in the Sui and Tang dynasties, although it was not widely used during these periods as most books were copied by hand. Early Chinese printing is rather like a lino-cut, the characters being carved on stone and hand-made prints taken from each block. During the Sung dynasty (A.D. 960-1280), printing techniques were improved and used extensively. This gave a great boost to acupuncture as far more books became available. Many of the pre-Sung books

suffered from repetition and confusion, especially over the location of various points and channels. These books were copied by non-medical calligraphers and this led to a great deal of confusion over the exact meaning of some of the characters in the text.

Chinese characters can change their meaning completely with a slight change in the text, and therefore a transcription error can easily change the sense of the text. The ambiguity of Chinese characters still poses a great problem in the translation of classical Chinese; for instance the character 'Ni' can mean to disobey, or to be in accord with someone. Exact translations therefore require the translator to understand the sense of the text and translate in accordance with this. The advent of more efficient printing techniques led to a more exact and faithful copy of the author's work, and therefore a clearer interpretation of the meaning of the characters. It is interesting to note that in Chinese philosophy all things have their natural opposites inherently within them (there is Yin in Yang, and Yang in Yin), and this is also displayed in the language as each of the characters may have a diametrically opposite translation.

The 'New' Bronze Model for Teaching Acupuncture Points
Because of the confusion that had gone before him, Wei-yi collected and collated all the information that was available to him in the eleventh century. He redefined all the points and channels and compiled an authoritative text called *Illustrated Manual on the Points for Acupuncture and Moxibustion on the New Bronze Model*. This text dates from A.D. 1026 and details the use of 354 points on the body. A vast amount of information is given about the location of the points, the method of needle insertion into each point, and the clinical indications for the use of specific points. There are also illustrations in the text to assist teaching and to act as a method of swift reference for the acupuncturist.

The Chinese were so impressed by this book that a statue was erected with the whole text on it! Two huge stone tablets were carved, some two metres high and seven metres wide, containing all the characters in Wang Wei-yi's book. These tablets stood in the capital of the Sung dynasty, now the city of Kaifeng in Honan province, where they could be read directly, or used like

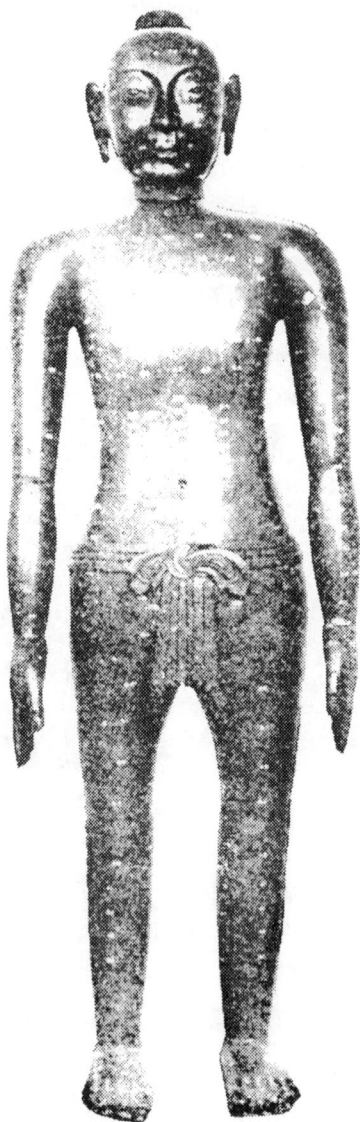

A reproduction of the bronze acupuncture model, first cast in A.D. 1443 (*Nanking Museum*).

a brass-rubbing to make a permanent copy of the book.

Wang Wei-yi also directed foundry men to create two life sized bronze models for acupuncture. These hollow models had on them the exact locations and names of the acupuncture points, and were used for teaching. Chou Mi, of the southern Sung dynasty, records in the *Historical Anecdotes* the way in which these models were used to examine students. The model was coated with wax and then filled with water, the student being given the name of an acupuncture point and a needle. If the point was punctured correctly the student was soaked as a fountain erupted from the model; failure to achieve this result meant that the acupuncture point had been missed.

In the Yuan dynasty (A.D. 1280-1368) the capital of China was moved to Tatu, now better known as Peking. The stone tablets and the bronze model were moved to the Imperial Medical College in Peking, but they were very worn and overused. Reproductions were therefore made in the mid-thirteenth century. Until fairly recently, the original model and tablets were thought to have been lost, but in 1971 five fragments of the original stone tablets were found in Peking, with much of the information still legible.

The Consolidation of Acupuncture Techniques

Acupuncture grew and developed over the next three hundred years; no new concepts evolved, but the old ones were refined. During the Ming dynasty (A.D. 1368-1644), Chinese society underwent the beginnings of an industrial revolution as paper mills, and textile and iron workshops began to emerge; Ming means 'bright' and this was undoubtedly a bright period of Chinese history. Acupuncture and related medical arts were encouraged, as were all the arts and crafts in China.

Li Shih-chen, one of the most outstanding physicians of this period, wrote and compiled the classical *Chinese Materia Medica* describing the pharmacology and botany of many indigenous herbs. He was also an expert acupuncturist and wrote a treatise on the *Eight Extra Channels*, describing their course and the indications for their use. Kao Wu collected the essential principles from many of the old acupuncture texts, editing the material into *A Summary of the Writings on Acupuncture and Moxibustion*. He soon found a great demand for this text and in

1537 he went further, compiling a similar but more detailed and complete text entitled *Essential Readings in Acupuncture and Moxibustion*.

Some of the observations in Kao Wu's book give us an amusing insight into the mores and morals of Chinese society. The Chinese seem very reluctant to allow a doctor to remove their clothing, and this habit is as widespread today as it was in the Ming dynasty. Kao Wu makes a point of disapproving strongly of the method of needling a patient through their clothing, but perhaps the fact that a patient can be diagnosed without removing clothing is one of the unsung benefits of Chinese pulse diagnosis!

Yang Chi-chou edited the *Compendium of Acupuncture and Moxibustion* during this period. Kao Wu's books were really short summaries for acupuncture students, but the *Compendium* was a complete collection of all the available material on this subject. It is copiously annotated and integrates the herbal remedies used with acupuncture and moxibustion. The *Compendium* was first published in 1601 and is still used as a reference text. Many of the source materials for this book have subsequently disappeared and consequently the *Compendium* represents an invaluable reference for those interested in acupuncture.

The Arrival of the Europeans

During the Ming dynasty contact was established with Europe, the earliest date being 1504 when the Portuguese landed at Macao. At about the same period, China's fleets began to visit India, Persia and some of the Arab states. Cheng Ho led the first recorded fleet of merchant ships to India in 1405, but it is certain that other Chinese merchantmen had travelled far afield prior to this date. The overland 'silk route' to China had been open for many centuries and merchants had for some time travelled into China and central Asia, following in the footsteps of Marco Polo.

With the advent of renewed interest in China, and also the wish of various European nations to 'discover and colonize' the non-European world, the Portuguese began to establish trading settlements in mainland China. With the traders went priests to convert the 'heathen'. It was through these priests, and also

Trade routes between China and the West from the first century onwards. Based on G. F. Hudson's *Europe and China* (Edward Arnold, London, 1931). By permission.

various physicians who visited China, that the idea of acupuncture began to filter through to the west. The Jesuits were particularly active in collecting and disseminating this information in Europe, but the process was far from one-sided as the Jesuits also introduced Western science to China. Dominique Parrenin, a missionary, translated a textbook of anatomy into Mandarin but this was banned from general circulation by the Emperor K'ang Hsi as he recognized that many of the Western concepts contradicted those of traditional Chinese medicine.

The Decline of Acupuncture and the
Rise of Western Medicine in China

The Ching dynasty (A.D. 1644-1911) was a time of chaos for the Chinese Empire. Western influences pervaded a war-torn China, especially during the nineteenth century when various Western nations were given 'spheres of influence' on the Chinese mainland. The Ching Emperors regarded acupuncture as 'a bar to progress' and in 1822 a government decree eliminated acupuncture from the curriculum of the Imperial Medical College.

During this period a great number of medical missionaries entered China to 'teach, heal and preach'. The medicine they practised in the early part of the nineteenth century had little similarity to the Western medicine of today, as there were no anaesthetics, antibiotics or sepsis. The concept that bacteria caused disease was only disseminated in the 1860's and 1870's, and therefore the missionaries had very little real medical skill to offer. Their main advantage was their understanding of the elementary principles of surgery.

The Confucian ethic had blocked completely the progress of surgery, as the Chinese felt that the dead must present themselves to their ancestors with a whole body. They were afraid to submit themselves to surgery in case they died and went to their ancestors with part of the body missing; surgery was therefore the province of the medical missionary and the basis on which their medical skills were accepted. The first full-time missionary was Peter Parker who worked in Canton. At first, the activity of the medical missionaries was limited by hostility, money and manpower, but as Western influence expanded the missionary work grew. By the 1920's, growth had reached a peak and there were some 550 hospitals and out-patient clinics spread over most of the provinces and cities in mainland China.

During this period the art of acupuncture was in decline. Many acupuncturists seemed to be no more than 'pavement physicians' with poor training. Their surgery was often the market place, their knowledge of traditional Chinese medicine was very limited, and their equipment was filthy and of poor quality. The majority of 'respectable' Chinese doctors were practising herbal medicine and massage, rather than acupuncture and moxibustion. In spite of its decline, and even at this low level, acupuncture remained the medicine of the masses. The Imperial denigration of acupuncture reflected not only the poor standard of practice but also the fact that some of the educated Chinese were looking to the West for progress. After the pneumonic plague of 1910 the Viceroy of Manchuria, Hsi Liang, remarked, 'The lessons of the epidemic are great . . . if railways, telegraphs and other modern inventions are indispensable to the material welfare of this country, we should also make use of the wonderful resources of Western medicine.'

Western medical colleges were set up by the missionaries, the first being in Canton. The missionaries translated Western medical books into Chinese and in 1886 began to print the *China Medical Missionary Journal* which was the first scientific journal in China. Another medical college was established shortly afterwards in Tientsin and there was a gradual increase in the number of Western-trained Chinese doctors. In 1929 the practice of acupuncture was outlawed in China; the passage of acupuncture has not always been smooth, even in China!

Communist Support for Acupuncture

In 1928 the Communist party of China was formed, under the leadership of Chairman Mao. A long guerilla war ensued and the Communist party finally took power in 1949. The Communists realized that there were little or no medical services in the 'liberated areas' and actively encouraged the use of traditional Chinese remedies to keep their troops on the move. These remedies were cheap, acceptable to the Chinese peasants, and utilized the skills already available in the countryside.

Acupuncture gained new momentum; in 1940 Yang Shao proposed to 'scientificize, "Sinocize" and popularize' traditional

Chinese medicine. During the early 1950's many hospitals opened clinics to provide, teach and investigate the traditional methods, the main research institutes being in Peking, Shanghai and Nanking. This renaissance of acupuncture, combined with a sophisticated scientific approach, has allowed the development of many new methods of acupuncture.

New Ideas Based on Traditional Chinese Medicine

Ear acupuncture is a particularly useful new acupuncture method. The *Ling Shu* states: 'The ear is the place where all the channels meet', and with this statement the Chinese justify the origin of ear acupuncture. The external ear is an homunculus, or little man (see page 117), with all the organs and parts of the body being represented on the ear. Puncturing the external ear at a specific point allows a disease to be treated in the body; for instance, if the arm is hurting then needling the arm point on the external ear will alleviate the pain in the arm.

Ear acupuncture has been used and developed by the French and the Chinese as a form of therapy and also, specifically by the Chinese, for acupuncture anaesthesia. Many people in the West think of acupuncture as being synonymous with acupuncture anaesthesia. The application of acupuncture as a form of anaesthestic is a relatively new development, and a direct product of the impetus given to acupuncture by the Communists. In 1958 acupuncture was first used by the Chinese to control post-operative pain and it then began to be used as an anaesthetic for simple operations. This technique was found to be effective and its use expanded quickly. In China it is now used for a wide variety of major and minor operations.

Acupuncture anaesthesia has many advantages including safety and swift post-operative recovery; however, it does not always provide complete pain relief, and whilst a small failure rate is acceptable to the Chinese it would not be acceptable in most Western societies. It is obviously better to use a site far away from the area of the operation when applying acupuncture anaesthesia, and this makes ear acupuncture the method of choice for anaesthetics.

The concept of the homunculus is one that the Chinese have developed further. There are complete representations of the body on the hand, foot, face and nose. Each of these represents a

Dental extraction with acupuncture analgesia.

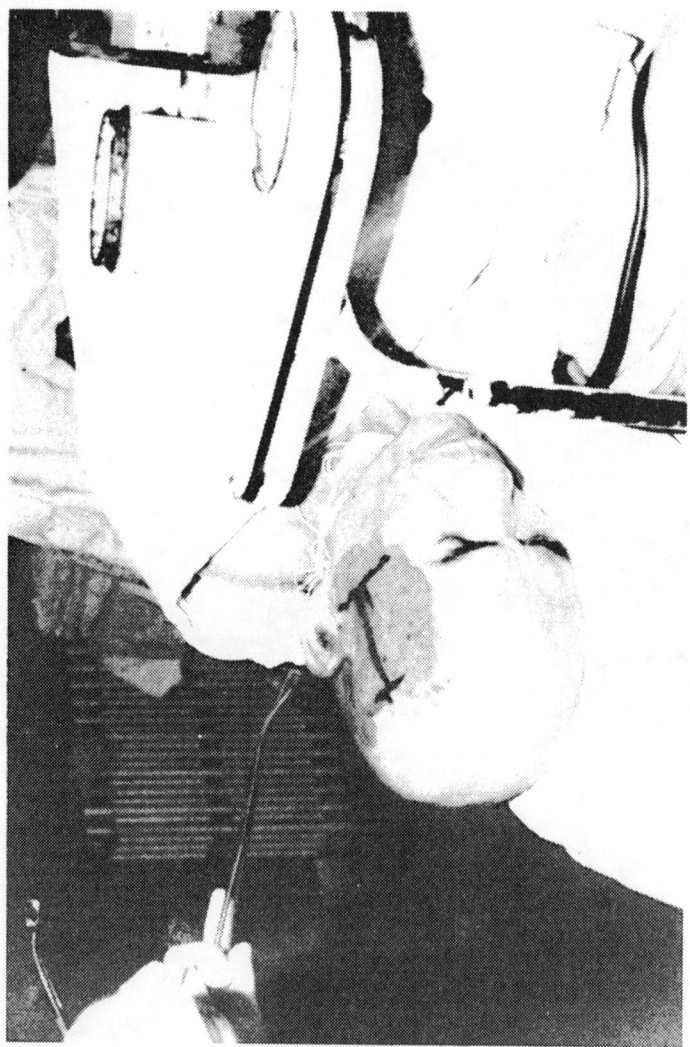

Removal of a brain tumour with ear acupuncture analgesia.

complete 'micro-acupuncture' system, capable of treating ailments throughout the body. Acute back pain can be relieved by stimulating the points on the hand that represent the back. Perhaps this can be equated with the fact that each cell in the body has the information potential to duplicate the whole human. The genetic material in each of our cells is exactly the same as the information in the cell from which we all originated, the fertilized egg.

New Ideas Based on Western Medicine

The Chinese have also applied a variety of Western techniques within the field of acupuncture. They have established research institutes and these, particularly in Shanghai and some other Chinese cities, measure up to any found in the West.

Scalp acupuncture, a technique invented in the last decade, is a direct development from the neuro-anatomy of the central nervous system. When the brain is damaged, in diseases such as a stroke, the scalp is stimulated superficially over the area of damaged brain. Although there is no clear connection between the nerves in the skin of the scalp, and the brain, this method does seem to produce an effect on the brain and the Chinese claim that they are able to alleviate some of the symptoms of a stroke with this procedure. Modern medicine has undoubtedly provided the stimulus for the development of this type of acupuncture.

Acupuncture points can also be treated by injection with ordinary injection needles, this method having been used in the West for some time although not called acupuncture. Tender, painful areas often occur in and around arthritic joints. Recent research work has shown that most of these 'tender points' are acupuncture points, and that injection therapy relieves the pain. Is it perhaps the needle insertion, rather than the fluid injection, that alleviates the pain?

Electro-acupuncture is the stimulation of acupuncture needles with small electrical currents, and its growth and development has been pioneered by the Chinese over the last thirty years. Throughout long operations, under acupuncture anaesthesia, electrical machines have been used to avoid prolonged, continual manual stimulation of acupuncture needles. Electro-acupuncture is now widely used in many acupuncture clinics,

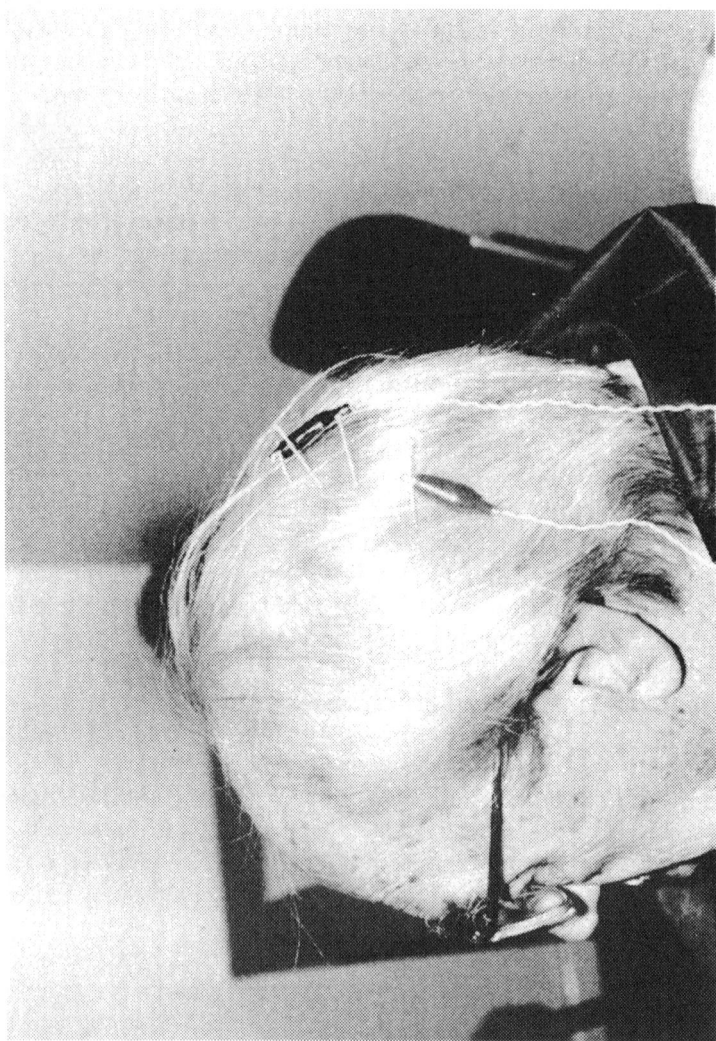

Scalp acupuncture being used for the treatment of a stroke.

for acupuncture therapy as well as for anaesthesia.

Contradictions Resolved?

The Chinese are well aware of the current scientific explanations of acupuncture and its mode of action, and through their research institutes they are contributing to this field. The cultural heritage of the Chinese has made it possible for them to accept the contradictions inherent in the practice of acupuncture; science versus philosophy. The concepts of traditional Chinese medicine allow the acupuncturist to approach and treat a patient. Eventually science will provide a logical explanation for these empirical findings, but, until such time as that happens, science and traditional ideas will both play an equal part in helping patients by the use of acupuncture.

7. The History of Acupuncture in the West

It is almost certain that acupuncture has been known and used in the West since the seventeenth century, but the first recorded use of acupuncture was by Dr Berlioz at the Paris medical School in 1810. He treated a young woman suffering from abdominal pain. The Paris Medical Society described this as a somewhat reckless form of treatment, but Dr Berlioz continued to use acupuncture, and claimed a great deal of success with it.

Acupuncture is not new to England, the first known British acupuncturist being John Churchill who, in 1821, published a series of results on the treatment of tympany and rheumatism with acupuncture. John Elliotson, a physician at St Thomas' Hospital, also use acupuncture widely in the early part of the nineteenth century. In 1823 acupuncture was mentioned in the first edition of the *Lancet*, and in 1824 Dr Elliotson began to use this method of treatment. In 1827 he published a series of results on the treatment of forty-two cases of rheumatism by acupuncture, and came to the conclusion that this was an acceptable and effective method of treatment for these complaints.

Ear Acupuncture
Those who travelled to China brought back information about body acupuncture. Ear acupuncture has been developed largely outside China. It is quite clear that there are some ancient Chinese manuscripts that mention the use of the external ear for acupuncture, but classical Chinese acupuncture applies to the

body rather than the ear. The detailed ear map that is now being used by most acupuncturists was developed by Dr Paul Nogier in France in the early 1950's.

Ear acupuncture was known to the ancient Egyptians. Ear cauteries have been found in the pyramids; these were used for burning or scarring specific ear points for conditions like sciatica. Hippocrates also mentions that the external ear could be used to treat conditions such as impotence.

In 1637 a Portuguese doctor, Zactus Lusitanus, described the use of auricular cautery for sciatica, and in 1717 Valsalva demonstrated the use of ear acupuncture for toothache. These early European and Middle Eastern experiments with ear acupuncture are a completely separate discovery; they have nothing to do with the growth and development of acupuncture in China. Sciatica seems to have been a disease that was particularly amenable to this crude form of acupuncture, and studies in the mid-nineteenth century indicate that 56 per cent of people who were treated with ear cautery for sciatica, obtained relief from their symptoms.

It was this crude form of acupuncture that interested Dr Nogier in the early 1950's. Some of his patients had received ear cautery and obtained relief from pain, and therefore Dr Nogier began to develop and investigate this form of treatment. He soon produced an ear map and since the early 1950's he has refined and developed this technique. One of his earliest findings was that if there was pain in the body then the equivalent part of the ear also became painful.

If the hand is painful then the part of the ear representing the hand also becomes painful when slight pressure is applied to the relevant part of the ear. If the painful ear point is punctured with a needle then the hand pain will be relieved. The picture of a pirate with a gold ear ring through his ear lobe is a well remembered childhood image; according to folklore the gold ring is supposed to increase the visual ability of the pirate, so that he can see ships to plunder before he is seen by them! Strangely enough, the ear ring usually seems to be placed in the eye point on the ear lobe.

Painful Points
Within the context of Western medicine, the development of

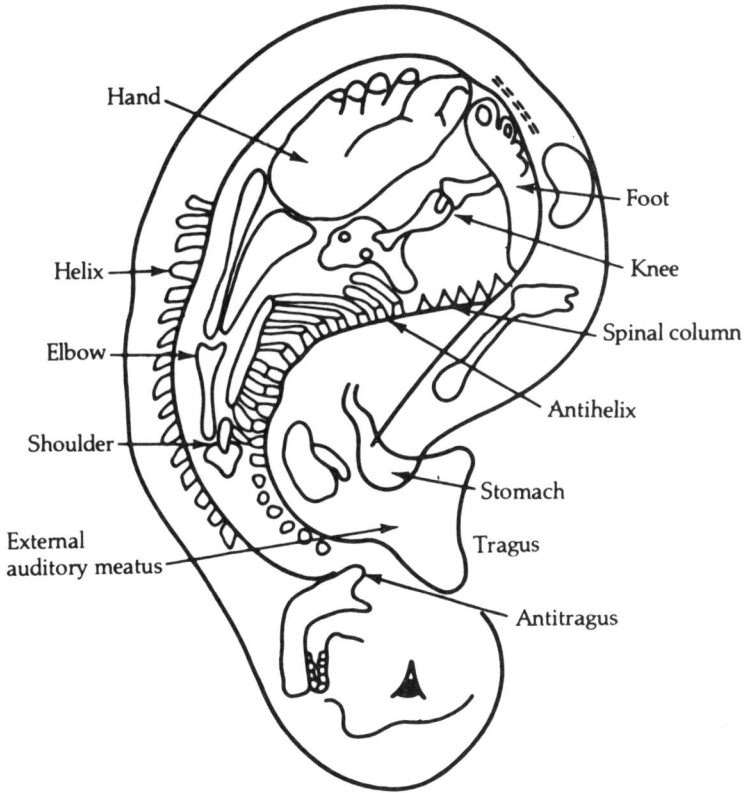

The representation of the body on the ear (after Nogier).

acupuncture points on the body demonstrates an interesting story of re-discovery. Over the last fifty years many Western physicians have discovered independently that pressing, stimulating or injecting various superficial body points can help to relieve pain. This is particularly true of muscular or rheumatic-like pains. These points are not necessarily at the site of pain, but often over distant areas. For instance, neck pain is frequently referred to the shoulder or arm and can present to the doctor as shoulder or arm pain. On close examination of the patient it is quite easy to define the origin of the pain, and to show that the neck is the cause of the problem. Injection, or stimulation of the painful points around the shoulder or arm, will often relieve the pain and free the movement of the neck.

These points have a variety of names, such as trigger points (for pain), or motor points. In 1977 Dr Melzack, who has been awarded the Nobel prize for his work in the field of pain, correlated these trigger points with acupuncture points, and found that most of the trigger points were already well known as acupuncture points. There are a number of explanations for the existence of trigger points but, as yet, there is no clear answer to this phenomenon. It is interesting to note that the Chinese realized this fact at least some three thousand years ago, and the *Ling Shu* summarises this approach when it says 'In pain, puncture the tender point'.

The Future

Acupuncture is now quite widely used in Europe and North America, both as a method of therapy and, in a few centres, as a method of anaesthesia. Operations with acupuncture as the main anaesthetic have been carried out in France and Austria, and the results have been comparable with those of the Chinese. Since its intimate contact with the Chinese in the 1950's, the USSR has also been using and researching into acupuncture, although the relationship between Russia and China could not be described as good. In 1972 a Russian researcher published work suggesting that acupuncture points were points of low electrical resistance on the body. He also found a network of low resistance points in both animals and plants.

The use of acupuncture in the USSR steadily increased during the 1970's and in 1972 acupuncture clinics were planned for all the major medical centres in the Soviet Union. The Russians claim they are using acupuncture for a wide variety of conditions such as asthma, stomach ulcers, raised blood pressure and angina, as well as for pain. In the West, acupuncture has been used mainly for pain relief. This is primarily because acupuncture for pain is easy to learn, and does not require a knowledge of traditional Chinese concepts in order to obtain results. The concepts of traditional Chinese medicine can seem alien and unacceptable to Western doctors and they are therefore rejected in favour of a simpler and probably less efficient method of treatment, in spite of the value of many of the traditional concepts. Some doctors practising acupuncture in the West are simply puncturing tender points as this seems a rational and logical approach.

Acupuncture has become very popular in North America since President Nixon reopened relationships with the Chinese. There are many research clinics evaluating the effectiveness of acupuncture, and also investigating the basic physiological mechanisms involved. The research output from North America is prolific and some excellent work has been done, much of which re-emphasises that acupuncture is an effective form of therapy for many conditions, especially pain, although it is not a guaranteed cure.

Over the last twenty years the West has developed a great deal of technological hardware which is now being applied in the field of acupuncture. The chapter on modern acupuncture techniques describes briefly the use of a variety of electrical machines and sources of stimulation, such as lasers and electro-acupuncture. Many of these techniques are still in their infancy and some will be rejected whilst others may prove to be important.

China is a poor nation without enough resources and trained manpower to research and develop acupuncture adequately. Until fairly recently few useful statistics were available from the acupuncture clinics in China, and most of the research into the basic mechanism of acupuncture had come from Western research institutes. Within this context it is probable that many of the major advances in acupuncture will come from the West rather than from the East.

Bibliography

Leith, Ilza (Ed.). *The Yellow Emperor's Classic of Internal Medicine*. University of California Press, Berkeley.

Lewith, G. T. and N. R. *Modern Chinese Acupuncture*. Thorsons, 1980.

Mann, Felix. *Acupuncture: The Ancient Chinese Art of Healing and How it Works Scientifically*. William Heinemann Medical Books.

Needham, J. *Science and Civilization in China*. Cambridge University Press.

——. *Celestial Lancets*. Cambridge University Press.

An Outline of Chinese Acupuncture. Foreign Language Press, Peking.

National Symposia of Acupuncture and Moxibustion and Acupuncture Anaesthesia 1979. Foreign Language Press, Peking.

INDEX

By the same author

Allergy and Intolerance
A Complete Guide to Environmental Medicine

George Lewith, Julian Kenyon and David Dowson

This comprehensive self-help guide to allergies, food sensitivities and chemical intolerance is written by three practising doctors who specialize in environmental medicine. The authors explain how and why the problems arise, and what we can do to help ourselves. If you are concerned for your own health and well being - or that of a relative - in an increasingly polluted world, you will find this book an invaluable source of information and guidance.

Demy 8vo 211pp   1 85425 067 1   £8.99 pbk

Modern Chinese Acupuncture
A Review of Acupuncture Techniques as Practised in China Today

G T Lewith and N R Lewith

An up to date view of acupuncture techniques as practised in China today, including new developments and advice on the treatment of some common diseases.

Demy 8vo 144pp   1 85425 088 4   £9.99 pbk